David has long had an interest in military history. He has had three books published on WW1 – a biography of Private Henry Tandey VC DCM MM, the organization of executions on the Western Front, and the story of the Shot at Dawn Campaign. In addition he has a novel published, *The Enemy at Home*, set in WW1.

Without access to John Stanfield's letters and other documents, this book could not have been written.

David Johnson

One October Day in Peking: The Japanese Surrender

Background Events and People Involved

AUSTIN MACAULEY PUBLISHERS™

LONDON * CAMBRIDGE * NEW YORK * SHARJAH

A CIP catalogue record for this title is available from the British Library.

ISBN 9781398479319 (Paperback)
ISBN 9781398479326 (ePub e-book)

www.austinmacauley.com

First Published 2022
Austin Macauley Publishers Ltd®
1 Canada Square
Canary Wharf
London
E14 5AA

Many thanks to John Stanfield and his nephew Mike Barrie.

Table of Contents

Introduction   13

1. Wednesday, the 10th of October 1945, in Peking   20

2. Major John Stanfield (Born 1920)   27

3. Special Operations Executive   39

4. Economic Warfare   56

5. Chinese Nationalists   61

6. Chinese Communists   71

7. British Army Aid National Archives   80

8. Japanese Army Atrocities   83

9. Operation Ichigo   96

10. Aftermath – Part 1   107

11. Aftermath – Part 2   112

Postscript   155

Appendix 1: Hong Kong War Crimes Trial (the 17th of Oct.
               1946 – the 14th of Feb. 1947)   157

Appendix 2: The Potsdam Declaration Issued on the Evening
               of the 26th of July 1945   166

**Appendix 3: Emperor Hirohito's Pre-recorded Radio
Broadcast to the Japanese People, Accepting the
Potsdam Declaration**   **168**

**Appendix 4: The Tripartite Pact Signed on the 27th
of September 1940**   **170**

**Appendix 5: Declaration by United Nations – the 1st
of January 1945**   **171**

**Appendix 6: United Nations General Assembly Resolution
2758 – the 25th of October 1971**   **173**

**Appendix 7: Smugglers, Spies and Dragon Slayers, Thursday, the 12th
of November 2020 | The National
Archives | On the Record, Podcasts**   **174**

Bibliography   **179**

Index   **181**

Every effort has been made to obtain the necessary permissions with reference to copyright material. I apologise for any omissions in this respect and will be pleased to make the appropriate acknowledgements in any future editions.

Photographs by Hedda Morrison – included thanks to Harvard-Yenching Library, Harvard University and Historical Photographs of China, University of Bristol.

The use of extracts from his letters was approved by Reverend John Stanfield.

"Formed in 1940, the Special Operations Executive was an underground army that waged a secret war in enemy-occupied Europe and Asia. Its agents demonstrated incredible courage and resourcefulness in their guerilla war. By working with resistance forces, they provided a boost to the morale of occupied societies."

"Unlike other special forces, SOE operatives usually wore civilian clothes. This meant they could expect to be shot as spies if captured. They also risked torture by the German Gestapo operatives (And the Japanese Kempeitai – Author's note) *trying to extract information."*

"The average life expectancy of an SOE wireless operator in Occupied France was six weeks."

(Quotes from the National Army Museum Website, November 2020)

Introduction

"All history relies on the evidence available to the author."
(Anthony Sheldon)

As the summer of 1945 had progressed, it became increasingly clear that Japan was to all intents and purposes facing either surrender or devastation as its Army, Navy and Airforce were effectively defeated. Allied bombing of Japan had left its cities devastated, as was its economy. Japan also faced having its islands invaded by the Allied forces.

*****

The theory surrounding the development of an atomic bomb had been published in journals before the war and was internationally available. Lieutenant Colonel Tatsusaburo Suzuki, himself a physicist, was the link between the Japanese Army and a small team that was working on the development of a Japanese atomic bomb. He submitted a report in 1940 that suggested that the disappearance of articles on nuclear fission from US technical journals meant the Americans were already at work on developing such a bomb.

> **Baron Kantarō Suzuki (1868–1948) was an admiral in the Imperial Japanese Navy, member and final leader of the Imperial Rule Assistance Association. At seventy-seven years of age, deaf and ill, he became Prime Minister of Japan from 7 April 1945 which was just four days after U.S. forces had landed on Okinawa. As Prime Minister, he privately favoured peace but publicly he urged the country not to surrender. His period in office ended on the 17th of August 1945 shortly after the Japanese surrender. He died of natural causes.**

However, the Japanese were confident that even if the United States was developing an atomic bomb, it would not be ready to deploy until after the war had finished; whereas Japan was confident that it could develop an atomic bomb and even had plans to drop one on Saipan in 1945. Saipan was, to the Americans, a strategically important island and the battle for Saipan started in June 1944 with the objective of gaining an airbase from which its long-range bombers and B-29's could reach Japan's home islands.

The Atomic Heritage Foundation explains on its website that there was an ultimately fruitless attempt by the Japanese to create an atomic weapon. The Japanese military invested in various efforts to research the potential technology, and indeed created the technology for uranium enrichment, but it was never enough to make a weapon, or develop the detonation technology that went into the American atomic bombs.

*****

In the build up to the Potsdam Conference, the Japanese Government had been putting feelers out to the Soviet Union, thinking that Stalin would give them more favourable terms in any peace treaty; but the other Allies knew that if Japan really wanted to end the war, then their only course of action was to approach the United States.

Meanwhile, the State Department in Washington was drawing up drafts of the surrender documents during which the issue of preserving the life and status of Emperor Hirohito caused much debate. While there was support for keeping Emperor Hirohito alive, notably Joseph Grew, former Ambassador to Japan and now Under Secretary of State, supported by others, there was some opposition to this, notably Assistant Secretary of State Dean Acheson, who believed that Emperor Hirohito should be punished.

The White House was similarly conflicted as some officials feared opposition from the public if concessions were made to those, including Emperor Hirohito, who had ordered the attack on Pearl Harbour and for the war that followed. This resulted in two versions of the draft surrender documents being taken to Potsdam. However, it would, in all probability, had been a mistake to punish Emperor Hirohito because it would have unleashed unrest across Japan which would potentially have tied down large numbers of Allied forces to control it and it might also have risked Japan coming under the control of the Soviet

Union which was preparing to invade Manchuria and increase its grip throughout Asia.

Throughout history, there are many examples of countries deciding to invade another country and topple its existing ruler(s) however, there is rarely a plan as what to do afterwards. This then results in large numbers of troops having to be deployed, and over a long period of time, to keep the peace leading to the problem of a civil war breaking out between opposing groups that materialise out of the population with their numbers increased by 'revolutionaries' from neighbouring countries, as was the case following the invasion of Iraq in 2003. Seventeen years later, American and British forces are still there.

*****

On 16 July, the United States had successfully tested their atomic bomb at Alamogordo in New Mexico. Knowing that the atomic bomb was now available, the Allied leaders, US President: Harry Truman, British Prime Minister: Winston Churchill, Clement Attlee, who became the next British Prime Minister during the conference, and Soviet Premier: Joseph Stalin, came together in 1945 at the Potsdam Conference, held at the Cecilienhof Palace, near Berlin, from 17 July to 2 August. Also present, were their Foreign Secretaries and other advisers. It was only seven days after the conference, on 9 August that the Soviet Union declared itself at war with Japan and on that same day, sent its troops into Manchuria.

The Japanese were given an ultimatum on 26 July, demanding 'the unconditional surrender of all the Japanese armed forces'. Failure to do so would mean, 'the inevitable and complete destruction of the Japanese armed forces and, just as inevitable, the utter destruction of the Japanese homeland'. One way or the other, Japan would pay the price for launching the war.

President Truman had told Joseph Stalin that the United States had a new bomb 'of unusual destructive force' but without saying that it was an atomic bomb. Why? Truman didn't want Stalin to know of this development but nevertheless, Stalin agreed at the conference that the new bomb could be deployed. In all probability, Stalin already knew it was an atomic bomb and this presented him with an opportunity to learn more about it. For the Americans, it also represented an opportunity to make the Soviet Union think twice about Soviet expansion, whether in Europe or Asia.

The Potsdam Conference Declaration was issued on the evening of the 26th of July 1945 (Appendix 2). There were divisions within the Japanese political and military hierarchy over whether to surrender or not, and on the following day, the Japanese Prime Minister, Kantaro Suzuki, responded by saying that the Japanese Government 'was paying no attention to the ultimatum'.

A leading Japanese newspaper laughed at the ultimatum with the headline *Laughable Matter*. As a result of the Japanese reaction, President Truman ordered the dropping of the atomic bombs, firstly to bring about the Japanese surrender and secondly, to bring the Japanese to the table, and to do so without Soviet assistance.

The first atomic bomb, named 'Little Boy' and weighing 4,400 kilograms, was dropped on Hiroshima on the 6th of August by an American Airforce plane named Enola Gay and killed an estimated 66,000 people. On the 8th of August, the second atomic bomb, named 'Fat Man', was dropped on Nagasaki, killing an estimated 40,000 people.

Early in the morning of the 10th of August, Emperor Hirohito accepted that Japan was beaten despite a group attending the Imperial Conference advocating that the war should continue, thereby avoiding the disgrace of surrender. Prime Minister Tojo tabled a response to the Potsdam Declaration which contained one condition that the Allies did not look to change the status of the Emperor. The final draft accepted the ultimatum from the Potsdam Conference but stated clearly, that the Japanese surrender was on the clear understanding that the Allied Declaration would not contain anything that would prejudice the status of the Emperor as Japan's sovereign ruler.

As a result, the Japanese surrender was announced by Emperor Hirohito in a pre-recorded broadcast at 10:50 a.m. on the 14th of August 1945. The language he used, classical Japanese, meant that what he said was not widely understood by his people at all levels of Japanese society. As a result, the Princes of the Imperial House were sent to the Japanese forces in China and Korea to tell them of the surrender. Shortly after the Emperor's broadcast, the Government of Kantaro Suzuki resigned.

The Potsdam Conference was to be the last Allied summit conference. At the conference, there was a high degree of harmony between the Allies but once the Second World War had ended, it was all change. The aims of the Western Allies would conflict with those of the Soviet Union, a state of affairs that still persists to this day, and perhaps more importantly, China.

Visitors to Berlin can visit the Cecilienhof Palace and see where the Potsdam Conference took place. Each national leader was allocated their own suite of rooms, although President Truman stayed at 2 Kaiserstrasse, and these contain the original furniture. Consequently, visitors will be taken to the suites occupied by Churchill and Stalin. The interesting one is where Stalin stayed, because, almost eerily, there is a smell of pipe smoke in the air, as if he had just left the rooms.

*****

On 2 September, the main surrender ceremony took place in Tokyo Bay on the deck of the US battleship, Missouri, which was the flagship of the Pacific Fleet, surrounded by two hundred and fifty Allied Naval vessels.

At the time of its surrender, Japan still had around four million troops stationed overseas and over the months that followed, the Allies accepted their surrender, and one of the surrender ceremonies was held in Peking, on the 10th of October 1945. One of the strange aftermaths of the surrender was the fact that the Allies remained dependent on the Japanese Army to maintain order in the countries where they were based. In China, once they had surrendered, the Japanese Army retained its weapons and was used to maintain order and to resist any attempt at a communist takeover. This situation persisted until the Chinese and other Allied troops arrived, at which point, the Japanese troops were disarmed and their equipment taken away. They were then taken to major ports to await their transit back to Japan.

Inevitably, some Japanese soldiers simply refused to surrender and they joined the various independent movements that were formed, for example: in Indo-China and the Dutch East Indies.

In 1974, Hiroo Onoda, a Japanese Army intelligence officer, was the last Japanese soldier to surrender when he was persuaded to leave the Philippine jungle. He had spent three decades in the jungle with three other soldiers refusing to believe that the war had ended with Japan's defeat in August 1945.

Over the years, Onoda and the others were responsible for the deaths of some thirty people whom they had mistaken for enemy soldiers. Their presence became known in 1950 when one of them handed himself in and was sent back to Japan. It is believed the second soldier also died in that year, while the third soldier was killed in a shoot-out in 1972.

Onoda was finally persuaded to surrender only when his former commanding officer travelled to his hideout in the Philippines to convince him that the war was really over. It was reported that Onoda wept as he handed over his rifle. He was formally pardoned by President Marcos, wearing his Imperial Army uniform of thirty years, for the killings that had taken place and then he went back to Japan. However, it wasn't the Japan that he remembered and so in 1975, he emigrated to Brazil where he became a farmer. He returned to Japan in 1984, where he died in 2014.

Military history books are full of aspects of both world wars, however, very little has been written about the Chinese involvement in World War Two, fighting on the side of the Allies or indeed the British involvement in China. China is a vast country and the Japanese invasion occurred in 1937, two years before the start of World War Two. The war was further complicated by the Chinese fighting amongst themselves, Nationalists versus the Communists, as well as taking on the Japanese.

This book therefore looks at just part of this story culminating in the Japanese surrender in Peking on the 10th of October 1945, and particularly, the characters, units and events involved. As Stanfield wrote: "Although this must have been the most brilliant and stirring surrender in the East, however, as communications were bad, it was hardly reported outside China."

As you read the book you will come across boxes:

> **The contents of which give you the bare bones of the box's subject which might motivate you to find out more about that individual or organisation.**

I am very grateful to Reverend John Stanfield for allowing me to draw heavily on his letters that he sent back to his family during the period 1941–1946. The then Major John Stanfield was an SOE operative in China and signatory to the surrender documents on behalf of the British Army.

1. Wednesday, the 10th of October 1945, in Peking

"Although this must have been the most brilliant and stirring surrender in the East, as communications were bad, it was hardly reported outside China."
(Major John Stanfield)

It was a beautiful, sunny day in Peking and for the tens of thousands of Chinese, including endless columns of schoolchildren who were making their way to the Forbidden City of the Ming and Ching Emperors of China, this was a day of double celebrations. Firstly, it was China's National Day, and secondly, the day had been chosen for the surrender of the Japanese Army which at the time numbered 500,000 men spread across forty-seven divisions.

It is impossible to know the range of emotions that they felt as they made their way to the ceremony, but they were likely to include joy that the nine-year war had come to a victorious end, pride in those who had fought the Japanese, sadness for those who had died, hatred of the Japanese for their oppression and atrocities and pleasure that their lives could now return to some form of normality.

*****

It had been decided that on the day of the ceremony, the small British Delegation needed to have a big car, as Stanfield wrote:

"I had to get a big car for 'British face' and my Chinese General Ho was very helpful and promised a big one. At 9 a.m. the big car turned up and was really 'big face'. A little trouble with the Union Jack was soon fixed and we proceeded to pick up Mr Lamb at the French Embassy."

The British Delegation, comprised Mr Lamb, a British Embassy official, Captain Stanfield (who was not yet aware that he had been promoted to the rank of Major), Captain Adrian Evans and Corporal Best and they set off travelling along the south wall of the Imperial City and as they drove along, they were greeted by much cheering from those who were making their way to the ceremony.

As the day progressed, vast crowds gathered in the courtyards of the Forbidden City. As the British and other delegations arrived, perspiring soldiers battled to clear a path for their cars to pass through the main fortress gates which took them through a 'fifty yard tunnel that had only been used by the Emperors until 1911 and out into the Forbidden City'. The delegations then left their cars and to the cheers of those there crossed the courtyard and climbed three flights of marble steps up to the Gate of Supreme Harmony. On both sides of the flights of marble steps, were terraces where the flags of the Allies flew, China, Great Britain, United States of America and Russia, and were packed with people cheering and clapping. As Stanfield later remarked, they 'felt for the moment, the focus of the universe'.

At the top of the steps was the Dragon Pavement behind which was the Grand Coronation Palace which contained the Imperial Dragon Throne. Stanfield has given a detailed description of the Palace:

"The pillars and walls are of deep crimson, the eaves and woodwork painted and decorated with golden dragons of the Imperial crest. The white marble balustrades and terraces were set off by the flags of the Allies in brilliant sunshine which gleamed on the Imperial yellow tiles of the rooves."

The ceremony was to take place on the Dragon Pavement where, for the last 500 years, the Emperors of China had come for the announcement of victories.

On the Dragon Pavement, a table stood on an Imperial Dragon carpet, and on the table were four sets of surrender documents. The documents were 'four concertina-like books, bound in yellow silk, and apparently made of blotting paper to take the Chinese brush writing'.

The Chinese authorities had allowed plenty of time for those delegations, who were to witness the ceremony, to arrive at the Dragon Pavement. Those who gathered there, all of whom wore the official red silk tabs, were described by Stanfield as "stately long gowned Chinese officials, modern Chinese Generals, American Marine and Airforce Officers, the British party mixed with civilian spectators of all nations", who strolled about, chatted and took photos.

The Dragon Pavement was guarded by Chinese soldiers on three sides with the fourth side looking out over the cheering crowds. As the time for the ceremony approached, a Chinese military band also arrived and took up its position. A Chinese General, who was leading the ceremony, then marshalled the official spectators into their allotted positions with their backs to the Coronation Palace with foreigners on the left and the Chinese dignitaries on the right. When all was ready, the spectators were then asked to 'salute or remove their hats as the War Zone Commander: General Sun Lien Cheng, came out of the shadow of the Palace into the brilliant sun, followed by his aides'.

One of the General's aides then called for the Japanese delegates to be brought forward. These represented the Japanese Army's forty-seven divisions in China. The Japanese were led by General Hiroshi Nemoto, accompanied by twenty officers. A murmur, quiet at first but slowly getting louder, from the vast crowds, accompanied the Japanese delegation as they walked down a two-hundred-yard corridor to begin climbing the three flights of marble steps. As they climbed the steps, the roar became a triumphal shout:

'Eight years of subjugation ended by the humbling of these officers about to surrender their swords on the spot where defeated enemies of China had surrendered their symbols of war for the last 500 years.'

General Sun Lien Cheng (1893–1951), had a long and distinguished career. After the Japanese invasion in 1937, he held many posts including Committee member of the Hebei Provincial Government (1939–40) whilst being the Commanding Officer Guerilla Warfare for the Hebei War Area. In 1942, he surrendered to the Japanese and then joined the Japanese Puppet Government. Then in 1945, he rejoined the Nationalist Government and became Commanding Officer of the 2nd New Route Army. In 1948, he surrendered to the People's Liberation Army and following an unsuccessful attempt to persuade General Lui Ruming to defect to the Nationalist Government, he was arrested and died in prison in 1951.

As they walked through what many commentators estimated to be a crowd of some 100,000 Chinese, it is once again impossible to tell what was going through the minds of the Japanese officers. Despite their military training and culture, they were human and therefore at least some of them would have been frightened, given their knowledge of the atrocities that had been carried out on the Chinese and other nationals. At the very least, they would have felt humiliated. If the Chinese Army had lost control of the crowds, it is quite likely that they would have been ripped apart.

When the Japanese delegation reached the Dragon Pavement, they formed a line in front of General Sun, came to attention and saluted before filing to the left where they remained at attention. General Hiroshi Nemoto, the General Commanding the Japanese Armies in China, was then called forward to sign the surrender documents. He walked to the table, sat down and then signed with a brush pen before returning to his delegation to watch General Sun sign the surrender documents.

The next order to the Japanese delegation was: "You will surrender your swords." Led by General Nemoto, they walked forward in single file, unhooked their swords and laid them on the table which Stanfield described as 'a very moving moment'.

The Japanese delegation then formed up once more, saluted and marched off to the right accompanied by the Chinese Military Band playing the Chinese National Anthem. The Japanese Officers would then have been taken to one of the Chinese ports to be shipped back to Japan.

General Hiroshi Nemoto (1891–1966) was serving as the Commanding Officer of the garrison of Mengjiang, now known as 'Inner Mongolia'.

During the Nanjing Incident in 1927, he was stationed at the Consulate General when it was attacked by the soldiers of the Northern Expedition. Nemoto suffered a bayonet wound but was able to escape by jumping from a second-floor window which caused him to have further injuries. He was, however, rescued.

In 1930, he was promoted to Lieutenant Colonel and led the China section, and in 1936, he became the leader of the Ground Army of Imperial Japan.

1930 was the year when a group of officers attempted a coup d'etat which failed, leading to the executions of those involved. Nemoto was thought to be part of that group, however, he was saved because on the morning that the coup d'etat began, he had overslept and therefore, hadn't taken part.

Following the Japanese surrender in 1945, he returned to Japan in 1946. He was aware that the Nationalists were on the brink of losing

control over China, particularly after Chiang Kai-Shek resigned as President in 1949. Nemoto pawned and sold some of his own possessions and with the support of others, raised enough money to enable Chiang Kai-Shek to set sail for Taiwan. Unfortunately, the ship sunk but Chaing Kai Shek was rescued and with American help, he reached Taiwan by air. Nemoto followed but was arrested on arrival. He was later released and Chiang Kai-Shek accepted his assistance particularly as the Americans withdrew military support. Nemoto successfully defeated the Peoples' Liberation Army (PLA) at the Battle of Guningtou. He finally left to return home in 1952, where he was punished, without prosecution, for going to Taiwan and assisting the PLA. He was eventually allowed to return to his home. On the 5th of May 1966, he was admitted to hospital, he was discharged on the 21st and suddenly died on the 24th.

It was then the point in the proceedings for the Allies to sign the surrender documents and when it was his turn, Captain Stanfield, escorted by General Ho, was brought forward to sign the surrender documents on behalf of the British Army.

*****

When the signing of the surrender documents was complete, and those on the Dragon Pavement were standing to attention, General Sun Lien Cheng saluted and then walked back into the Coronation Palace where in its 'dim pillared depths, stood the huge dragon throne'. The Allied representatives and other dignitaries then followed him into the Palace to drink numerous toasts to each other. Eventually the moment arrived to leave and this still felt like a triumphal procession as the 'crowds still clapped and cheered as we made our way through the vast courtyards and palaces out from the fifteenth into the twentieth century'.

Later Stanfield wrote:

"One felt drained of emotion, the scene had been too picturesque and colourful for reality, the acres of golden tiles, deep crimson walls, marble balustrades, the waving crowds. Such a scene can happen only once, and this surrender in China's five-hundred-year-old Forbidden City must have been for

China, the Supreme moment of Japanese defeat." He went onto say that "the setting and the day combined to make it as colourful and awe-inspiring as any in China's history".

*****

One of the ironies of the Japanese surrender was that the Japanese Army remained in control of Peking protecting it from the Chinese Communists until the Allies could produce enough troops to takeover and as a result, the Japanese were then disarmed and eventually shipped off to Japan.

Later, Stanfield took time to reflect on the potential aftermath and had written:

"Actually, the war out here seems to be about to start again. The Japs are still fighting the Communists and the local Chinese are at the mercy of the Japs, but the Japs are behaving quite well. The American troops have already landed at Tientsin and will be here shortly. So long as there are strong foreign troops here to keep order, things will be okay, immediately they go there will be civil war. Here everything seems peaceful, the Japs are keeping a bit low, but they are still worried about their future. They are selling their goods, as they won't be allowed to take much to Japan. Swords are fetching quite low prices."

*****

On the 29th of November, Stanfield "found out that they have made me a Major!" And from the 16th of September, the signal had come through from Chunking. It stated:

"To Captain Stanfield from Col. Bridge. 28/11 Have just received from Headquarters orders to promote you to Acting Major. As to the exact date from which promotion will take effect, this is not definitely settled, but in my opinion will date from 14/9. I have to advise you as above and send you, my congratulations."

Stanfield's next problem was getting the insignia for his new rank: "Fortunately, Adrian Evans had two sets of crowns, one on his great coat and he gave them to me for my uniform service dress."

In the weeks following the surrender, Stanfield received invitations to many luncheons, teas and dinners:

"I had a wonderful lunch at the Swiss Consulate. It was a Chinese meal deluxe but served on silver plates & dishes, which were an immense weight…I attended two dinners with dances after, at the French & Spanish legations. Having been here quite a while, my face is known…the French are very anxious to entertain…there are a number of the younger generation, in great demand…I suppose I have managed to get in on the last of the old Peking legation life."

Stanfield also attended a Chinese wedding: "We arrived at the correct hour of 2:00 p.m. and waited till 4:15 p.m. for the bride to appear."

2. Major John Stanfield (Born 1920)

"I was interviewed, and when I suggested the Navy, I was told that with my Science education, I would be better used in the Army Royal Signals."
(Major John Stanfield)

John Stanfield left school in July 1939. At that time, his school was planning to join the German Schools Exchange at the end of that term but it had to be cancelled because of the likelihood of war breaking out. The German school party had already visited England and among the pupils had been 'Goering, nephew of Air Marshall Goering: Hitler's number two. Ribbentrop's (German Foreign Secretary) son was also in the party.'

In September, Stanfield went to Liverpool University to study for a science degree. He had not long started his second year when in November 1940, he received his call-up papers. At his interview, prior to him joining up, he expressed an interest in serving in the Royal Navy, however, he was told that with his science education, it would be better if he served in the Army and in particular, the Royal Signals.

*****

In January 1941, his papers arrived and he reported to the Ladysmith Barracks, home to the Manchester Regiment, at Ashton-under-Lyme. As 2365115 Signalman Stanfield, he started his basic training where he 'joined a squad consisting largely of Welsh miners and marched up and down the square and over the Yorkshire Moors'. This was to be the start of his journey from Britain to South Africa, then to India and finally, as part of the SOE in China.

One month later, he was posted to the Royal Signals Training Camp at Catterick to begin training as a wireless operator. The training involved more exercises around the Yorkshire Moors in "wireless trucks, as well as line laying, operating at twelve words a minute, and a lot of electrical theory and mechanics of wireless sets. We also learnt to drive cars, lorries and motorbikes."

In a letter dated the 27th of February, he wrote that he had looked around the camp, "There is a shopping centre, a NAAFI and a YMCA fairly close, but the nearest town is Richmond, Darlington is the nearest large town."

Stanfield was a very regular letter writer to his family and in a letter dated the 27th of January 1941, he wrote: "Issued with vast quantities of kit, 4 blankets, 2 battledress suits, 1 overall, 3 pairs of socks, 2 pairs of boots, 2 pairs of long inners, jersey, gloves, 2 towels, but not yet a tin hat or a respirator, but they will come."

Throughout his training, Stanfield enjoyed playing rugby, soccer and cross country running and his letters are full of the games he played and the races he ran:

"Battalion sports were on Saturday. Our Company against the Training Battalion and the 152 OCTU, where I hope to go. We came second and beat the OCTU, not bad for one company. I came 2nd in 220 and long jump, 3rd in 100, three medals. I spoilt my best jump by leaning back. The 220-winner started off about five yards ahead of anyone else. Still, I won't complain."

It was during this time that he was interviewed as to his suitability to be an officer. On the 27th of February he wrote that "the Major sent for me yesterday and said he would send in papers which had come from the Joint Recruiting Board for a commission". Stanfield knew that it would be several months before his commission was approved. By the 9th of March, Stanfield was an IM (Instrument Mechanic,) which was the most specialised job in the Royal Signals and the most highly paid.

Stanfield did not enjoy all elements of his training and particularly was not enamoured of the billets and the food. He didn't enjoy the key operating training, writing: "I am getting a bit tired of all the key operating, buzz-buzz in your ears all the time. I am not doing any E (electricity) or M (magnetism) as I did well enough in my first exam." Later that month, Stanfield was busy with tests on E&M again, map-reading, air defence, and gases among others.

*****

Officer Cadet Stanfield entered the Officer Cadet Training School at Catterick on the 25th of July 1941 and was issued with 'white shoulder tabs and cap bands'. In October he wrote, "We have started wireless and line work alternately, learning the insides of wireless sets and how to lay telephone cables."

In preparation for his passing-out parade, scheduled for January 1942, Stanfield wrote on the 7th of December:

"I am getting my first uniform fitting from Austin Reeds! Quite an expensive business. The SD (Service Dress) will cost £11 and also the great coat. I ordered a middle quality. I am left with £12 for the rest – cap, hat, mac, boots, shoes, shirts etc."

In a letter on the 16th of December, he outlined the financial impact of becoming an officer:

"If all goes well, our commissions should come through next month. This will mean a hefty jump in my finances. I am on the absolute basic 2/6d a day. As a 2nd Lieutenant in the Royal Signals, my pay will start at 11 shillings a day, plus my extra Royal Signals pay of 1/2d a day, what wealth!"

On the 17th of January 1942, Stanfield was commissioned as a 2nd Lieutenant in the Royal Signals and was posted to the 53rd (Welsh) Division Signals stationed in Wem, Shropshire.

Stanfield sets out in his book, *War Letters Home 1941–1946*, where the Signal Sections fitted into the Army's organisation:

"Divisional Signals have Signal Sections in the Brigades and the Royal Artillery Regiments of the Division. Each section is a unit attached to the Brigade or Artillery Regiment but run by Signals. I was given experience in different sections and then appointed OCE Section Royal Signals attached to the 81st Field Regiment Royal Artillery. The Division moved south to Kent."

The Division, which moved in April 1942, was based in Sutton Valence, near Maidstone, and Stanfield writes about the make-up of his section:

"In my section, I should have 1 Sergeant, 1 Lance Sergeant, 2 Corporals, 4 Lance Corporals. I am below strength, so it is a job to get everything done. I have also to train Gunner Regimental Signallers, which takes time and NCO's which I can't spare."

Stanfield's section was involved in field exercises such as crossing rivers and setting up wireless stations together with laying and relaying telephone cables.

On the 1st of October 1942, Stanfield was promoted to Full Lieutenant and thereby earned an additional two shillings a day. Shortly after his promotion, he was forced, he hoped temporarily, to give up playing rugby and soccer due to 'an ankle that keeps turning over, but I am still able to do some running'.

The 1st of December brought another move, this time to 160 Brigade HQ Home Forces as the 2nd Signals Officer which had 50 signals personnel with more due. At the end of 1942, "I, with others, was posted to form Signals HQ Wireless Operating Sections to go abroad." Stanfield was in the "Third Holding Battalion to train a Wireless Operating Section of 40 men in preparation to go abroad". He was expected to go with them.

*****

February 1943, saw Stanfield and the three Wireless Operating Sections receive their kit for overseas operations and then were transported to Glasgow by train where they 'boarded a magnificent ship', SS Strathaird, which was one of the P&O 'Strath' class ocean liners. Their destination was South Africa.

Stanfield was responsible for censoring his men's letters. In one of his own letters, he wrote:

"There was an absolutely magnificent happening in the dining saloon this morning at breakfast. As you may gather, the weather is very pleasant and the port holes are open. Just as we were finishing breakfast, along came a wave a little larger than usual and it decided to investigate a port hole in the dining saloon. The people there were drenched, also a couple of eavesdropping stewards. You have never seen such surprised-looking faces."

At the beginning of April, the ship arrived in Capetown where they then spent four days' leave before moving on to Durban where they were to stay for two months.

On the 6th of April, Stanfield wrote about the Clairwood Camp where they were based:

"I find this place a bit expensive, but as I get three shillings a day extra, I am not so badly off." It was quite hot weather at the camp and he went on to write: "I am doing quite a bit of training with my boys but not enough. The atmosphere is not conducive to working hard."

Two days later, he wrote:

"Life here is like a holiday. The day is as follows: breakfast about 7:30. Parade and training from 8:30. All except those on duty can then go into town where food is very good and fruit most plentiful; swimming in the sea, or baths in the afternoon; films at night and so to bed."

There were frequent trains into Durban and it was on one of these trips that Stanfield's section suffered its first fatality when one of the men fell between the platform and the train. "A horrible shock to us all. I had to identify him.

Fortunately, we had Padre Bennett who was well known to us and he was able to help the lads."

*****

In May, Stanfield and the three Wireless Sections joined a convoy for India that eventually arrived in Bombay. From there they were then sent by train for two days up to the north of India. To try to make the heat on the train more bearable, ice was loaded onto the train. On the way they stopped at Dehera Dun, which is north of Delhi where Stanfield was able to kit himself out at the Officers' Shop. He was able to get sheets, khaki cloth for making bush shirts and shorts, and underclothes.

Stanfield and his men were in a camp at the foothills of the Himalayas and in a letter home on the 29th of June, he set out the daily routine:

"Reveille for the men is 5:00. I manage to struggle on parade at 7:15. Breakfast about 8:00. Work 9:15–1:30. Afternoon siesta from 2:00–5:00. Recreational training period 5.00–7.00."

On the 11th of July, he wrote: "I am writing this about 8000 feet up in the mountains, where we have been firing rifles. Unfortunately, it has just started raining and we are confined to our trucks."

In this letter home, Stanfield informed his family that he had been appointed Assistant Adjutant, which he was not happy about. "It is a stooge's job and I am very sorry to lose my 72 Operating Section. There may be advantages though and I am not shouting until I find out. I suppose in a way it is not altogether a demotion."

A week later, Stanfield wrote:

"As I told you in my last letter, I have been appointed Assistant Adjutant. I am just taking up the reins. I suppose a bit of administration will be a good thing, but certainly more boring than having a section." Things were no better when he wrote again on the 8th of August: "I am getting tired of my job as assistant adjutant but I suppose I will have to stick it."

On the 10th of August he wrote:

"I have started Chinese! A doctor in the mess wants to go to China. He has started to learn and has a number of characters and words written down. However, even I could tell his pronunciation wasn't Chinese. He is passing on the written, while I try to teach pronunciation, we have no textbook."

In a letter dated the 19th of September, Stanfield was sent on a training course to Jhansi and he wrote: "This training course is for junior officers from all over India, Indian and British." The conditions in Jhansi were tough:

"Today is very hot. I am sitting at my table underneath the automatic Punka with only pants on. The prickly heat comes and goes in waves. Whenever I go out into the sun, the heat hits me. Even the flies have stopped bothering to any extent. This is an extraordinary country; you can rarely be comfortable."

Such was the frequency of sightings of snakes, scorpions and 'the largest spider ever' that Stanfield took care when going to bed that his mosquito net was well tucked in under his mattress.

Stanfield had not enjoyed his time as an assistant adjutant and before going to Jhansi he had asked to go back to a section and so on his return, he was posted to Section 75 "with two and a half hour's notice. I am now at another spot, doing a temporary job."

Much to Stanfield's excitement, he was given a motorcycle which he said 'was good for his job'. It was necessary to enable him to visit his section which was dispersed away from the main camp. "This morning, I had a glorious run on my bike (to my dispersed groups) partly to pay them."

On the 11th of October, Stanfield wrote home that he 'had just had a letter by dispatch rider about leave'. One of the camp doctors who was also due some leave had invited Stanfield to go with him to Nani Tal which was a hill station six thousand feet up the Himalayas. It had a lake with yachts and boating. By the 17th of October, Stanfield was informed that his leave would start on the 25th for ten days: "It should be a good trip with one of the doctors, Captain Warburton-Smith, a good chap."

Stanfield persisted in his learning of Chinese and on the 17th of October, he wrote: "I had a Chinese lesson with the doc. I stayed the night for it. There is an exam in most languages, if you pass, you get reimbursed. For Chinese, I believe 500 rupees. A bit of a carrot." In a letter dated the 19th of October, he went on to say that his Chinese "progresses slowly, I know a few characters. I find it hard to get the tones right, also practicing conversation with oneself is difficult."

Stanfield's leave was welcome and did him good. On the 27th he wrote: "I have been up here a day and a half and am feeling ten times better than I was two days ago." He, and Captain Warburton-Smith, stayed in an officers' hostel which, at times, also served as a convalescent home.

On the 9th of November, Stanfield was back from leave but found himself moved to another tented camp outside Delhi. In his letter, he described the camp as follows: "It is very much more dusty, which covers everything. The tents are not quite so good, as we have not got electric lighting yet. We rely on paraffin lamps."

*****

Stanfield was then posted to GHQ India where he served in the South-East Asia Command Signal Office (SEAC). In a letter dated the 14th, he noted that "since being here, my Chinese has lapsed". So far, his time in the Army had yet to place him on the front line and on the 25th he wrote: "With all the fighting in Italy, and elsewhere, we seem to be out of things." He was not particularly happy at this time, writing that he and the other subaltern he shared a tent, "grouse together about staff and what we would do to get somewhere. That we are vegetating etc."

> **South-East Asia Command (SEAC). At the Quebec conference of August 1943, it was decided that a joint Anglo-American command should be established for the prosecution of the war in Burma, Malaya and Indo-China.**
>
> **In November of that year, the command came into being, and was designated South-East Asia Command, with Admiral the Lord Louis Mountbatten as Supreme Allied Commander South-East Asia.**
>
> **The British operational command under SEAC was Allied Land Forces South-East Asia (ALFSEA), previously known as 11 Army Group. 11 Army Group was reorganised in November 1944 to include Northern Combat Area Command (mainly American and Chinese troops commanded by American officers), 14th Army and Ceylon Army, and redesignated ALFSEA. SEAC ceased operation on the 30th of November 1946. (National Archives)**

By the 29th, his Chinese was progressing slowly and he wrote: "I have a copy of the 214 radicles, I now know 1 and 2 stroke characters." (A Chinese radicle is a graphical component of a Chinese character under which the character is traditionally listed in a Chinese dictionary.)

He wrote on the 3rd of December:

"I have just had a narrow squeak when driving in on my motorcycle. I followed a car when entering a speed trap and was pulled up. I had a clear conscience and thought it was a driving license check. I was horrified when they said I was doing 37 mph. I pointed out that I was following a car which was certainly not doing 30. After some argument, my name was crossed off. Just then who should turn up but our Chief Motor Transport Officer who had also been gonged! Only he did not get off. When I left a Despatch Rider was caught and more were piling up."

By the 12th of December, Stanfield had managed to get hold of a Chinese dictionary from a local shop for 19 shillings and wrote that "the task overawes me. How to distinguish between all the tones? I am plodding on with radicals and phonetics. Any tips Dad?"

In a letter written on the 17th, Stanfield revealed that he was in charge of the SEAC Signal Office in GHQ India, "with a variety of switchboard personnel, my own section, an American detachment, RAF detachment and Indian Army Women Operators, all in the magnificent Central Government Buildings of India." As a result, he had been moved to a new camp which he described as 'an improvement'. In terms of quarters:

"We each have a tent with a brick floor and a bathroom with shower. It is a relief to get off the dust which was all pervasive in the last place. There are electric fittings but as yet, no bulbs. They are in short supply, important black-market items, about 7 shillings each."

At the start of 1944, the weather was cold and Stanfield wrote on the 19th of January: "I have a fire in my office this morning. I would not have thought it possible in India," adding:

"I have a delightful American sergeant working for me, who calls me 'Loootenant', which is rather a trial for my sobriety. He has a very pleasant accent and is most polite. On the whole they are a very polite nation and have a nice way of saying you're welcome."

On the 23rd, he wrote that he had rearranged his tent.

"I have maps around the walls and mats on the floor. I hang my clothes on a wire between the tent poles. The door is covered by a 'chick', an open bamboo curtain, which rolls up. The floor is brick so, on the whole, I am nicely fixed."

In the same letter, he describes having to turn out the guard at 0400 hours:

"It is an effort to get out of bed, partially dress, put on a coat, pop on a motorbike and make myself unpopular with an inoffensive guard. I realise how unpleasant it is to get abruptly woken at 0400 in the morning while having a nice unofficial sleep on guard duty. Still, at that time one is inclined to be a bit crotchety, which may be good for discipline."

Stanfield experienced a similar moment a few days later which he recounted in a letter dated the 6th of February:

"I found myself Orderly Officer again, without a motorbike. I had to turn out the guard at some awful early hour. I borrowed a bike, which was one I had not ridden before, an American model 'Indian' with controls and completely different. It was quite funny to hear me trying to start and trying to get into gear. Once in, I could not change the gear and went along like an aeroplane. I got there, but the guard (and probably the whole camp) was well warned in advance. I then needed a push start. I shall never get that model bike."

In a letter dated the 16th, he wrote that he was on a course with his unit:

"It was a short toughening-up course that culminated in a 32–mile march in full battle dress and fully armed." Stanfield was worried about his feet. By now the weather was a lot warmer so the plan was to start at 1900 hours, march for seven hours, 'stopping for a bite', and then 'marching on a further 12 until we get in'.

The course involved mainly marches leading up to the 32–mile finishing march. "We started with a ten–mile march, but our feet were so bad after that, that we had to take things easy for a day or two and work up." When the final 32–mile march started, it was raining and thundering and "we were in the middle of the 'Chota Monsoon' (small monsoon)." Because of the weather, the march started the following morning before dawn and the first phase involved a 19–mile trek before a break for 'tiffin' when, "we were glad for an hour to be on something other than our feet."

Many of the men by that stage were suffering from blisters, and some were unable to walk any further and so were sent ahead by truck. The men who were still standing then started off on the remaining miles. The blisters got worse and "By this time, our feet were hurting beyond pain and most didn't know and didn't care, if there was anything left below the ankle." However, they made it and enjoyed a day to laze around and rest.

On the 8th of March, Stanfield wrote home asking: "Could you send brown Kiwi polish, unobtainable here."

The 19th of March saw Stanfield take a day off to visit the Taj Mahal which he found impressive. "The Taj is most lovely, but the marble is so white that it hurts the eyes to look at. Not much there but empty rooms and tombs, all in white marble. The gardens are well laid out."

Stanfield had been unable to take any photographs because his camera had been stolen when his batman had forgotten to lock his room. On his return from the Taj Mahal, he learnt that:

"They have caught the thief, a waiter came and said the police sahib had got my camera, and there it was on the table, with the Inspector, the prisoner in chains, and most of the mess staff. His mistake was trying to sell it for eight rupees. Another officer had his watch and wallet stolen, also recovered. The thief was a dhobi man (washerman)."

*****

By the 26th of March, Stanfield was making plans to get away from India writing:

"I went to the Postings Office and asked the lady Captain in charge, about possibilities for Signal Officers in China, as I knew some Chinese (only about five words). She arranged for me to see a Colonel Jackie Knott, Chief Signal Officer of Force 136, who had a pleasant interview with me and said he would see what he could do." Unbeknown to Stanfield, the Captain "put my name forward to a certain organisation which wanted Signal officers in China", which eventually turned out to be his route into the SOE. "I went to see the Chief Signals Officer in Force 136. We had a pleasant chat and he said he would see what he could do."

Although Stanfield's camera had been recovered, by the 7th of April, it had still not been returned to him and he wrote that it was "still at the police station. I have a summons to appear at court on Monday, so I hope to collect the camera." The weather was getting warmer as "summer is here, I am sorry to say, still only between 90–100 (degrees), there is another 20 to come before we are through." Stanfield was still hoping for a posting to China as 'office work just about kills me'.

On the 14th of April, Stanfield had gone to court only to find that the case was adjourned, however, he still hoped to have his camera returned on the 19th.

*****

The 23rd of April, saw Stanfield posted to 3 Company, Army Group Signals, Rear HQ, 11 Army Group, SEAC. He wrote that his: "official address is as above, but you had better keep an eye on telegrams which I will send when my address changes (China in the offing). I am glad to say that my plans are gradually bearing fruit, I hope that my Chinese primers and dictionaries will soon be of use. I am waiting for a posting order now."

On the 24th, he wrote that he was "about to have a Chinese lesson from a Chinese. I hope I can understand something of what he says."

By the 13th of May, Stanfield had been promoted to Captain and had been posted to Military Establishment No. 9 Meerut, India Command and wrote to his parents to tell them: "I will be unable to mention shop in the future."

*****

On the 12th of June, Stanfield had joined M.E. India Command in Force 136 Training Centre in Meerut and he wrote: "Little free time recently. We knock off between 1 and 4, but it is so very hot, that it is hard to get down to anything. This heat reduces reactions and faculties about 50%." By the 25th, he was writing: "It has become horribly hot and sticky. I am covered with prickly heat. Most unpleasant, in my hair and neck and tummy etc. This is the hardest thing to bear."

Part of the training involved Stanfield learning:

"A little about the special wireless suitcase sets that were to be sent by various means behind enemy lines. First the A3, and then the newer, more powerful B2. These were crystal-controlled working from mains or six volt batteries. They worked great distances if the right frequencies were chosen, China-India. I also learnt the various ciphers and codes, the double transposition lower security and the unbreakable one-time pads. In Meerut there were wireless operators from many different eastern countries being trained to be sent, some by air drop, some by submarine, and any other way possible."

Force 136 was the cover name for the SOE in India, Burma, Sumatra, Siam and later, China. Force 136 was primarily created to supply local resistance forces in enemy territory, although it occasionally carried out sabotage operations. However, South-East Asia presented some unique challenges to SOE. It was a vast area to cover, with many islands, challenging physical terrain and very diverse populations and languages.

It was formed to liaise with resistance groups in the Japanese-occupied countries, recruiting indigenous people to assist in sabotage and information gathering and it was commanded by British Officers.

*****

In July, Stanfield was posted to China:

"Urgent signals from Major Philip Smith, O.C. SOE Signals in China, expedited my move to China. After too short a time, learning all the necessary SOE Codes and Ciphers and special wireless sets, I trained down the 800 miles to our SOE station in Calcutta. I then flew over the 'Hump' (the Himalayas) in a Dakota 1000 miles to Kunmimg in South-West China. This is 6000 feet up with a large lake surrounded by mountains, our SOE headquarters in China."

3.   Special Operations Executive

"SOE, the Special Operations Executive, was a small tough British secret service, a dirty tricks department, set up in July 1940."
(M.R.D. Foot)

The Special Operations Executive was formed by the British Prime Minister, Winston Churchill, after the evacuation of Allied soldiers from Dunkirk and the fall of France. Churchill's attention had been drawn to the way that the German Wehrmacht had used specially trained units of paratroopers and others, to infiltrate behind enemy lines, to sabotage and disrupt their enemy's lines of communication and supply, with the effect of confusing and throwing off balance the enemy's forces.

It was formed on the 22nd of July 1940 under the Minister of Economic Warfare, Dr Hugh Dalton. At that point, Germany was in the ascendancy and it was felt necessary to, 'continue the fight in occupied countries by underground secret means' which turned out to mean, 'anything to disrupt the enemy, to target armament sites, communications, bridges, railways, organising guerilla forces with local resistance forces'.

Initially, the SOE was formed with three branches:

SO1 – For propaganda

SO2 – For subversion

SO3 – For planning, although this branch was disbanded in the early days of the SOE.

Dr Hugh Dalton (1887–1962) was a British Labour Party economist and politician who, under the direction of Winston Churchill, formed the SOE. Following the General Election of 1945, the new Prime Minister, Clement Attlee, appointed him Chancellor of the Exchequer nationalising the Bank of England in 1946. In 1947, he was forced to resign after budget details were leaked to a journalist and was replaced by his long-time enemy: Stafford Cripps. In 1948, he was brought back into the Government as Chancellor of the Duchy of Lancaster and also served as Minister of Town and Planning. Dalton was made a life peer in 1960 and died in 1962.

The SOE had previously worked out of 2 Caxton Street, London, but then moved to 64 Baker Street. Its newly appointed head was Brigadier Colin Gubbins and because 64 Baker Street was relatively small, he and his staff had based themselves in two flats in Berkeley Court which was opposite Baker Street Station. Gubbins had made his name by writing three pamphlets, based on research that included a review of those activities from around the world together with his own experiences. The first was *The Art of Guerilla Warfare*, the second *Partisan Leaders' Handbook*, and the third was *How to Use High Explosives*. These pamphlets went on to form the core of SOE training for active resistance groups in the field. Upon later establishing SOE, one of the key security features introduced was 'Commit as little as possible to writing. Memorise if you can. If you must carry documents, select what you must carry. Burn all secret waste and carbons'.

Gubbins was a military man who, initially, like many other senior officers, saw little benefit in subversive operations, but he finally came around to the idea that, if properly coordinated with regular operations, then guerilla warfare indeed had a decisive contribution to make. Such was the secrecy surrounding the SOE that very few people were even aware that it existed. To those in the know, it was known as the 'Baker Street Irregulars', after the location of its Headquarters, 'Churchill's Secret Army' or the 'Ministry of Ungentlemanly Warfare'. For security reasons, the SOE was referred to as the 'Joint Technical Board', the 'Inter-Service Research Bureau', or the names of fictitious branches of the Armed Services. The Headquarters occupied two family flats off Baker Street.

Major General Sir Colin Gubbins (1896–1976). In November 1940, he became acting Brigadier and, at the request of Hugh Dalton, was seconded to head up the Special Operations Executive which had recently been established to coordinate all action by way of sabotage and subversion against the enemy overseas.

Gubbins was given three main tasks: to set up training facilities; to devise operating procedures acceptable to the Admiralty and Air Ministry; and to establish close working relations with the Joint Planning Staff.

He was also given the task of setting up the secret Auxiliary Units, a civilian force to operate behind the German lines when it looked as if the United Kingdom was about to be invaded.

When the SOE was closed down in 1946, Gubbins was not offered another military post and so retired from the Army. He then became managing director of a carpet and textile manufacturer.

Gubbins also had an effect on Ian Fleming. Prior to World War Two, Fleming worked for the Foreign Office and in early 1939, he had been posted to Russia and his cover was that he was a reporter for The Times newspaper. With war looming, he was tasked with assessing Russia's armed forces. In July 1939, the newly appointed Director of Naval Intelligence, Rear Admiral John Godfrey, was looking to recruit an assistant and Fleming's name was put forward and Godfrey appointed him.

Again, there was a difference between Fleming's official post, Lieutenant in the Special Branch of the Royal Navy Reserve, which later turned out to be the role that a certain James Bond had held. With a post in the Naval Intelligence Department, Fleming acted as the Admiralty's liaison officer with the SOE. Once again, his official post acted as a cover because the SOE did not officially exist and therefore its agents and missions did not exist either which meant that anything was possible, as would be the case with James Bond.

Fleming liaised with the SOE's Operations and Training Director, Brigadier Gubbins, who was known within the SOE as 'M'. Not surprisingly therefore, when Fleming's James Bond books were published, 'M' was the Head of MI6 and Bond's boss.

*****

All SOE operatives were required to sign the Official Secret Act. New recruits were given in-depth training in unarmed combat, firearms, sabotage, parachuting and wireless techniques. In addition, research and development stations were set up near Welwyn in Hertfordshire, where scientists and technicians worked on specialist weapons, forging documents, sabotage equipment and camouflage materials. The SOE could not have operated without appropriate radio communications and so it developed a wireless set that weighed less than 40 lbs. and looked like an ordinary suitcase. By 1945, there were some 13,000 SOE operatives of which 3,200 were women.

Initially, Churchill ordered the SOE to 'set Europe ablaze', but over time, its reach extended to India, Burma, Malaysia, the East Indies and most countries as far as China. The creation of the SOE was opposed by the Head of the Secret Intelligence Service, Sir Stewart Menzies, who made his views known on numerous occasions saying that the SOE were: 'amateur, dangerous, and bogus'. Menzies' major concern was that the SOE would disrupt the activities of his own agents.

Sir Stewart Menzies (1890–1968) was Chief of MI6, the British Secret Intelligence Service (SIS), from 1939 to 1952. During that time, he grew the wartime intelligence and counter-intelligence operations and supervised the work of Bletchley Park.

Opposition to the SOE also came from the RAF Bomber Command, on the grounds that having to loan aircraft for clandestine missions was risking the loss of planes and aircrew, thereby affecting what it saw as its mission to win the war by bombing Germany. However, Churchill believed in the SOE and therefore, it survived. The following is taken from the National Archives:

"Shortly after the Special Operations Executive (SOE) was set up to engage and harass the enemy in Europe, preparations for guerrilla war in the Far East were begun and terms of reference for an SOE group in Singapore were settled by SOE Headquarters in November 1940. Known as the Oriental Mission (OM), it was to operate under the C-in-C Far East. A Singapore headquarters under a civilian, Valentine Killery, was established in May 1941, but his operating methods met with strong objections from the local military authorities, and this, together with the rapidity of the Japanese advance, meant that it was short-lived and its achievements relatively limited. It was wound up in mid–1942.

*****

A separate special operations organisation in India was established in May 1941, initially to cover countries to the north and west. It was expanded eastwards after the Japanese invasion brought India into the war zone and the OM had ceased to exist. The India Mission, known subsequently, as Force 136, under Colin Mackenzie, operated on the authority of the Viceroy and the C-in-C. Although the directive followed the lines of that for SOE operations in Europe, the Far Eastern theatre had nothing in common with that of Europe, either in local (native) perceptions of who constituted the enemy, or in the vast size and physical character of the territory to be covered and its remoteness from London. Its operations were therefore of a very different nature."

*****

However, when the SOE started to operate in China, it became just another 'secret service' that struggled to coordinate its work with the other intelligence services. The Chinese Intelligence service, headed up by Dai Li, worked more closely with the American Sino-American Cooperation Organisation (SACO) which did not get on with the other American intelligence services. Supposedly this was down to Dai Li being arrested at Kai Tak Airport in Hong Kong which resulted in him spending a night in prison. He was only released and allowed to continue his journey after considerable diplomatic activity.

American Sino-American Cooperation Organisation (SACO) was a US Naval Group that operated behind the Japanese lines in China and consisted of 2,964 American service men. In addition, it worked with Chinese guerilla groups, rival groups and individuals.

It provided weather reports from areas occupied by the Japanese to the Allied navies and their air forces and helped rescue downed airmen. It is claimed that some 71,000 Japanese were killed as a result of its activities.

(Sino American Cooperative Organisation US Naval Group China Veterans)

William Donovan visited Britain in July 1940, as President Roosevelt's Special Envoy to personally evaluate its military and intelligence capabilities and assess its chances for surviving the German attack. Donovan was also briefed on the SOE.

Eventually, the China Branch of the OSS was set up under the command of 'Wild Bill' Donovan and came to an agreement that it would co-ordinate the activities of the Chinese Intelligence Service and SACO. This was despite the fact that Donovan viewed South-East Asia and China to be an American operational theatre and therefore, in his eyes, America took precedence.

> **William Donovan (1883–1959), often referred to as 'Wild Bill', was an American soldier, lawyer, intelligence officer and diplomat, who served as the Head of the Office of Strategic Services (OSS), which in time became the Central Intelligence Agency, during World War II. He is regarded as the founding father of the CIA, and a statue of him stands in the lobby of the CIA headquarters in Langley, Virginia. Donovan was sent to China by President Roosevelt in 1941.**

However, this agreement unravelled when Donovan decided that the OSS would operate separately in China. In 1942, Dai Li was convinced that the OSS would enable both the American and British intelligence services to bypass him.

> **Dai-Li (1897–1946) was Chiang Kai-shek's spymaster known to the Chinese Nationalist as their leader's 'claws and teeth' and to the British as the 'Chinese Himmler'. He controlled all the spies in China and in those countries that had Chinese communities. In 1946, he was killed in a plane crash and rumours suggested that either his death was arranged by his Communist counterpart, Kang Sheng, or the OSS given that he was aboard an American aircraft.**

At a banquet held on the 2nd of December 1943, Donovan informed Dai Li that if he would not work with the OSS then it would act without him being involved. Dai Li's response, which was shocking to say the least, was to say that he would kill any OSS operatives who acted outside his command. In response, and equally shocking, was Donovan's threat to then kill Chinese generals. The next day, Chiang Kai-Shek intervened reminding Donovan that China was a sovereign country and that he should act accordingly, but still there was a lack of co-ordination between the different intelligence services and therefore they could not agree on common policies in China.

The American Ambassador, Clarence Gauss, stated at one point that there were fifteen Allied intelligence services acting in China and they were 'completely uncoordinated to the delight of the Chinese'. (Mitter, R, 2014). At its simplest, this was a basic example of a lack of leadership and as a result, they all felt that they could act individually.

Another example of ineffective leadership was the rivalry between General Stilwell and General Chennault, which will be discussed later, which was also causing problems. Stilwell did not get on with Chiang Kai-Shek while Chenault did, and Chennault argued that the key to beating the Japanese was air power while Stilwell argued that it was the Army that would bring victory.

> **General Joseph Stilwell (1883–1946) served in India, Burma and China in the Second World War. During the course of the war, he went from hero for leading a column, travelling on foot, out of Burma when chased by Japanese forces and then to zero for units suffering from disease to be sent into combat.**
>
> **He sadly had a habit of falling out with people – Chiang Kai-Shek and General Chenault to name but two.**

*****

The American Airforce, under General Clair Chenault, was based in Kunming in South-West China. General Clair Chenault (1890–1958) had retired from the US Army in 1937 and had then been recruited by the Chinese Nationalist Leader, Chiang Kai-shek as his aviation adviser and trainer. At that time, the Chinese Air Force could do very little to stop the Japanese Air Force. Although the Chinese Air Force had some 500 planes, only 91 were airworthy and Chenault's first task, therefore, was to rebuild it. He did this by recruiting pilots and mechanics from the USA, after President Roosevelt had reluctantly, and these eventually came to be known as the Flying Tigers, the first mercenary air force in history. These pilots adopted Chenault's tactics of taking the fight to the enemy and achieved a good combat record against the Japanese at a time when the US Airforce was concentrating primarily on high altitude bombing.

Chenault was able to fund the rebuilding of the Chinese Airforce thanks to nine million dollars from a private corporation, the Chinese Defence Supplies.

After America entered the war, the Flying Tigers became part of the US Air Force in the 14th China Air Task Force. Chenault was recalled to active duty in 1942 and within a week, he was promoted to Brigadier General and in 1943, to Major General in command of the 14th Air Force. Chenault had promised President Roosevelt that he would defeat the Japanese in China and during this time, he had repeated clashes with General Joseph Stilwell who repeatedly failed to approve Chenault's requests for more planes. He finally returned to the USA in 1945.

On Saturday, the 20th of December 1941, ten Japanese bombers took off from Hanoi Airfield carrying 500–pound bombs. Their plan was to fly some three hundred miles to bomb Kunming. The aircrew would have been relaxed to the extent that it had been decided that a fighter escort was unnecessary because the Chinese Airforce had neither fighter-planes nor anti-aircraft guns. As they approached Kunming, they were shocked to see four fighter planes heading towards them, although at that time they had no idea that these planes were part of the Flying Tigers Squadron. The fighter-planes closed on the bombers and opened fire with their machine guns, bringing down four of the bombers. The remaining bombers had little option but to turn tail and jettison their bombs in an effort to get back to Hanoi but only three made it back.

Despite the fact that the Flying Tigers never had more than fifty pilots, as the above story shows, they had no problem dealing with the Japanese Airforce destroying 297 planes with another 240 unconfirmed kills, and 40 planes destroyed on the ground. The Flying Tigers, in return, suffered four pilots lost in combat, six lost to ground fire, three died in training exercises, three killed in Japanese bombing raids and three taken prisoner.

After Pearl Harbour, the Chinese became one of the allies fighting Japan. However, since Japan had invaded China in 1937, China had limited resources and so had gradually retreated from its coastal regions leaving Japan in total control of those areas. Consequently, the only way of helping China was from the air with limited material and resources. Those resources included special forces of which SOE formed a part under the auspices of Force 136.

Though this resulted in many positive outcomes, there was also a downside as the Malayan Peoples' Anti-Japanese Army (MPAJA) was, in effect, a largely Chinese Communist entity because many of its fighters were ethnic Chinese. The MPAJA was disbanded in December 1945 at which point, it was supposed to return Allied supplied weapons to the British Army. However, little was returned and indeed went on to be used by the Chinese Communists in its own subsequent guerilla campaigns against the Chinese Nationalists.

Entry to China by the Allied forces was not easy as Japan controlled the Chinese coast and the Burma Road had been cut when the Japanese invaded Burma. The only way left to cross into China was by air from India which meant flying over the Himalayas, known as the 'Hump'. The main airplanes used were Dakotas and these had been stripped down with aluminum bucket seats installed down each side. The flights took six hours. Stanfield described the flight as follows:

"The trip over the Hump in a Dakota was fine. I hardly felt at all sick. It was an amazing experience, we went so high over the Himalayas that I was too drowsy to be very interested in the experience. I have hardly been able to bring anything with me and am restricted in my garments. I hope my tin trunk will follow shortly."

The SOE, under its commanding officer, Colonel Kenny Brand, was based at a signal station some fifteen miles from Kunming along the side of a lake at Shishan. Stanfield described Kunming as follows: "Kunming was the main centre to exit China by air and all British refugees, who had been pushed out of their stations by the Japanese advances collected here."

The base had been set up by Major Philip Smith in the Church Missionary Society compound, which included a hospital, together with its Matron, Miss Tindall. By July, Stanfield was the second in command of the SOE China Signals, under the cover of being attached to the British Army Aid Group and wrote describing the base as: "15 signal personnel living in the lower house and Philip and me in the small top house with the wireless room." He went on to say, "we had a motorcycle to take the signals to Kunming Office." The base also provided communications for the Ministry of Economic Warfare office. "We had four large pet dogs in the compound which were the best possible guard, all were well bred, two were bull terriers. We had a Chinese cook. Philip and I fed in the house."

By the end of the war, Churchill was held in high regard with an approval rating in Britain of 83%. To everyone's surprise, just three months later, on the 5th of July 1945, he lost the General Election. The other Allied leaders were amazed and particularly Joseph Stalin who was sure that Churchill could have 'fixed' the result. Britain had elected a Labour Government and the new Prime Minister, Clement Attlee, closed down the SOE in January 1946. This was despite General Eisenhower praising the important contribution that the resistance forces had made to the Allied victory. SOE's problem was that with no war to fight, they had finally lost out to the opposition from the other British intelligence services.

Eventually, Captain Stanfield was sent to US Airforce's forward base at Kweilin, some five hundred miles away where he became, 'officially, the Signals Officer for the British Army Aid Group. The journey took four days in a British Military Mission truck using roads that 'were totally mud and stone' and all the way Stanfield was alert for bandits:

"I am quite prepared to battle with bandits all the way down, but none turned up. I suppose when one has a Sten gun and a revolver, it is rather unfair on a poor bandit, with only an old musket and a sword."

Stanfield described the journey 'through magnificent country and mountains':

"The area was mostly inhabited by the Miau tribes and the women were very brightly dressed. Unfortunately, goiter was endemic. We stopped at night in the inns, where we unrolled our bedding rolls onto the string beds provided. Usually there were plenty of bed bugs waiting to join us, so the new DDT powder was used to discourage them. We ate the Chinese dishes which were mostly very good. The plain wooden tables and benches and mud floors were usual."

Soon after Stanfield arrived, Major Smith returned to Kunming leaving his second in command in charge of BAAG Signals which looked after communications with agents each side of Hong Kong and back to Kunming.

By the 27th of August, Stanfield was still making do with the clothes he had been able to bring with him:

"My one pair of shoes shows it, but it will last a month or so, if not, I shall have to take to my one pair of boots." He then went on to write: "With the

Japanese advance from Central China it livens things up and adds to difficulties from my point of view." His job was to keep all the wireless links open to all agents and back.

By the 3rd of September, Stanfield was still in Kweilin but fully aware that the Japanese were advancing, causing him and his men to retreat first to Ishan and then on to Dushan. Of the retreat from Kweilin, he wrote on the 17th of September:

"There is no security being broken in saying that Kweilin has been entirely cleared out. It was a ghost city when I left. Fires were burning at various points. The Japs were not in the city, but I expect it will be besieged in a few days. Every civilian ordered out of the city. The few trains with more people on than anyone would believe possible. The last train out of Kweilin had the roofs entirely hidden and people hanging everywhere else, even under the carriages. American airfield demolition going on. Fires in the city and large columns of red smoke. The truck journey was interminable, but very interesting; three officers and 20 Chinese staff. We had ferries to cross, waiting long hours in queues. At one place, we built a ford in a shallow part and managed to get the truck across."

By the 22nd, Stanfield had arrived in Ishan and he wrote:

"We have no light at night except oil and candles. The Japs have taken most of the coal production, and railways etc. find it difficult to run. In fact, it amazes me that anything functions at all, particularly the incredibly decrepit Chinese trucks."

The journey was uncomfortable and because the electricity supply had been cut, the wireless sets needed batteries. On one occasion, Stanfield travelled by truck to an American airfield to see if he could salvage a battery. The Americans were blowing up a lot of the airfield's stores and Stanfield was fortunate to get 'an enormous accumulator, which was fully charged, and half a drum of airplane oil to keep our trucks going'.

The trucks were a problem and Stanfield's:

"Was very difficult to start and all the lights, except one side light, did not work. We struggled into a village on one side light, the truck was almost impossible to start. In the morning we had to light a fire under the engine to warm it up, with a little petrol to prime it. When the engine started, the accelerator spring went. We could accelerate but not decelerate. So we had to tie a string to the pedal to pull it back each time. The fuel pump gave up, so the only way was to put the tank on the roof of the cab to work by gravity."

However, they made it to the wireless station at Yishan which was set up in a graveyard just half a mile from HQ. "It was just a lath and plaster hut. My Chinese operators worked up to Kunming and Kweiyang and down to the agents near Hong Kong. The conditions were terrible as far as sanitation and health were concerned."

The 14th of October found Stanfield in Dushan preparing the Rear Headquarters for the next move which turned out to involve, 'another crock truck'. Three days to do 200 miles. By the 27th, Stanfield was back in Ishan and by the 5th of November, he was ill:

"I have not kept anything down except a couple of boiled eggs for the last two days. Afraid my private fears have come true. I am a horrible yellow. No wonder I wasn't feeling so good. Unfortunately, there are no doctors around. I have taken my case of Jaundice in hand and I am pretty well starving myself, not that I have any appetite. The one thing I remember is that one keeps off fats, so I am eating boiled fish and boiled chicken with army 'dog' biscuits with some local honey."

Despite feeling ill, Stanfield still had to ensure all the wireless links and stations stayed in touch during the retreat back to Kunming.

By the 14th, the evacuation back to Dushan was completed and "the Japanese reputed to be in our old place Ishan. We had 24 hours' notice to get out quickly. Unfortunately leaving a lot of our stuff."

On the 16th of December, Stanfield was back in Kunming after a 500–mile road journey. The journey back had been difficult:

"It is unbelievable to see the chaos on the roads when refugees come in force. All the old trucks in China get stuck at the same time and make a completely impenetrable barrier. One block consisted of 500 of the most aged charcoal burning buses imaginable (with gas bags on the roofs filled with gas from charcoal burners on the back). It was only by pushing a couple over the cliff and other drastic means that any trucks got through."

In a letter home on the 23rd, Stanfield wrote about the refugees:

"Talk about refugees, thousands and thousands. You feel sorry for them until you join the milling mobs. Imagine a road jam involving up to 1,000 of the most decrepit trucks in existence, mostly running on charcoal gas producers, on mud roads and everyone, at least, doubly overloaded. Quite as effective as blowing up the road! However, the Japs seem to be going back now."

On the 31st of December, Major Philip Smith was recalled to SOE Headquarters in Kandy, Ceylon, for six weeks leaving Stanfield in command of the China Signals.

Early in the New Year, on the 10th of January, Stanfield wrote home that he had: "missed the European fighting. Still, I am happy in my job here." On the 25th, he wrote:

"One officer's rations which always seems to come is a bottle of whisky and a bottle of gin a month. There is a big demand (from Americans and I have swapped mine for an American raincoat come wind coat etc. A very nice, expensive garment."

It was at this time that Stanfield's men lost contact with the French agents in Indo-China:

"The French were rapidly being swamped by the Japs and urgently asked for supply drops. The American Airforce had agreed to provide planes and were standing by for a message from the Indo-China agents to give place and time. Nothing arrived and the French officer kept asking, as it was essential to go, before the moon vanished. After a search, the message was found in the wrong page of the dispatch book. The moon had gone and the drop was impossible. As the OC said – someone will have to be shot or it must be discreetly forgotten."

Major Smith was back from India by the 1st of February, but he would be 'off again soon to Chunking'. When Stanfield wrote next, on the 22nd, Major Smith was still away and the first paragraph of the letter concerned Colonel Kenny Brand:

"I am glad that Kenny Brand (Colonel) has written to you. We were all sorry when he left, he must be about 50, but he took us for some good walks in the hills. He was our SOE chief in Kunming. He had to return as his business partners were all dying. He could not have taken more than a week returning."

On the 16th of March, Stanfield wrote that: "I have now got a stooge! By name of Allen King (Lieutenant). He is a good lad aged 22, so I feel quite patriarchal." By the end of March, Major Smith had returned. By the 16th of May, Stanfield had flown 500 miles to Chunking, the wartime capital of China, and in a letter, he described the city:

"Chunking, if you forget the heat (which isn't easy), is a pleasant place on the banks of the Yangtsi, which is a good half mile wide here and very fast flowing. It is liable to rise 100 feet. The first impression one gets is of steps, with lines of coolies carrying great buckets of water up hundreds of steps. Smells compete with steps for first impressions. It is the war capital of China and has a very variegated crowd of people. All the embassies and missions."

The 27th saw Stanfield preparing to go 1,000 miles by road to Sian. He travelled with Captain Adrian Evans (SOE Captain Intelligence), Chinese General Ho (Chinese Director of Military Intelligence), and his staff in a jeep, trailer and a British military truck. Also travelling with them was Signals Corporal Best who was to train and oversee the Chinese wireless operators to work the B2 suitcase sets. Stanfield had to have an authorisation with Chiang Kai-Shek's seal on it to allow him to travel.

On the 26th of June, Stanfield, accompanied by General Ho, Guo (Ho's secretary and honorary colonel), Lai Ping Huen (W/T mechanic) two Chinese wireless operators (Chinese captains) and a Chinese servant called Lai, travelled by jeep and trailer to establish two wireless stations on the Yellow River bend, opposite the Japanese positions: "I had two complete wireless stations with batteries, steam and hand worked battery chargers, a drum of fuel and all our bedding."

The first part of the journey involved travelling 100 miles on a train, with the jeep and trailer having been loaded onto an earlier train ready to meet them at the end of the line at Wha Yin in the Yellow River bend. There followed a challenging road trip in the jeep to an old fort where they met General Albert Wedemayer, American Commander in Chief, and Marshall Hu Zung Nan, War Zone Commander. After enjoying a meal, the party continued along a worsening road but eventually, "we were welcomed to the village nearest to 'Sparrow' with a deputation."

> **Marshall Hu Zung Nan (1896–1962) was a general in both the National Revolutionary Army and the Army of the Republic of China. He was one of Chiang Kai-Shek's most trusted generals and following the Nationalists retreat to Taiwan in 1949, he became the President's Military Strategy Advisor until his death in 1962.**

The whole village was lined up to meet them although the 'village had suffered considerably from shelling'. Stanfield and his men put up an aerial and tried to get working 'the 18.00 sked (wireless schedule)' but failed to get an answer. Stanfield wrote after he had walked through the village and to the watchtower overlooking the Yellow River and the Japanese lines that 'at that time, I must have been the furthest British soldier not in captivity'. There were strategic points where agents could cross the river with information about Japanese movements:

"If the agents had to walk to deliver the information, it would be totally out of date. I also got two walkie talkies, just produced, so that the agents could speak across the river. The Yellow River is a vast river, it was miles across. There was a $10,000 reward by the Japs on the head of any allied officer. This was the first time I had a personal bodyguard, which was often a nuisance and an embarrassment."

On the 28th, the 08.00 wireless schedule still didn't get a response although they had "fixed the steam generator, looks like a little toy steam engine, the boiler had to be fueled by the residue of the cotton crop". Later that morning, Stanfield was introduced to two men "who were to take the walkie talkies across the river. I tried to explain the workings to them."

At 18.00, Stanfield made another attempt to meet the wireless schedule but without success, largely due to the batteries being flat. This was followed by a battery charging competition with a hand generator. "Every agent had a go and between the lot raised the Specific Gravity of the battery from 1180 to 1190! I cannot think they will be prepared to turn the generator by hand for three-four hours everyday." Later in the evening they sat and listened to the machine guns on the other side of the river.

General Albert Wedemayer (1897–1989) was a United States Army commander who served in Asia during Second World War from October 1943 to the end of the war. Previously, he was an important member of the War Planning Board which formulated plans for the Invasion of Normandy.

After serving as deputy commander of the South-East Asia Command under Admiral Lord Mountbatten (1943) he was appointed chief of staff to General Chiang Kai-shek and commander of U.S. forces in China (1944–46).

The following morning, the wireless was operating which meant that Stanfield and his party, minus those manning the wireless station, were able to leave to set up the second station named: 'Crow' via the railhead at Wha Yin. By the time they arrived, the jeep needed to be refueled but they had no petrol. A telephone call by General Ho to Sian received an assurance that the petrol would arrive by 17.00, except when it arrived, there was only ten gallons which would not be enough. Finally, Stanfield "went to an American OSS (equivalent to SOE) who was running a little wireless station. He gave me as much petrol as I wanted."

The party left at 09.00 on Sunday, the 1st of July, leaving Adrian Evans behind as he had orders to return to India. Although it was 'glorious morning', the roads still proved problematic; however, they reached Hancheng at 19.00. After returning from the bath house to his quarters "an agent arrived with Jap papers. I was given the best room. It has good maps and pins showing the agents' lines of communication."

Once again, there were problems setting up the wireless but on the morning of the 3rd, it was working and so it was packed onto a jeep which Stanfield drove up into the very steep hills where they left the vehicle and walked the last mile before returning to Wha Yin.

Stanfield was busy, but as he wrote, "I am tired and I am not able to write about it," adding, "my first priority is to get some money from the Army to re-educate myself. The Army is a short-term activity, which doesn't satisfy long term aims. At present, it is very interesting. I dare say in time you will hear of my activities."

After establishing the two wireless stations, Stanfield went with General Ho and the SOE'S Colonel Bridge to Marshall Hu Zung Nan, the War Zone Commander's Headquarters in Sian to plan the guerilla army to go behind the Japanese lines which was steadily advancing.

On the 11th of August, Stanfield heard the news:
"Of the dropping of atomic bombs, on one of my wireless sets last night. The end has certainly come suddenly – but I don't blame the Japs with Atomic Bombs buzzing around. The Chinese newspapers are saying that the crater is nearly a mile deep!"

Consequently, the planning for the guerilla army came to an end.

An important element in SOE operations was Economic Warfare, which was conducted by a businessman named Walter Fletcher.

4. Economic Warfare

"Garrulous, old, impulsive, vague, obese,
Only by luck not known to the Police."
(Sir Walter Fletcher)

The Oxford English Dictionary defines 'Economic Warfare' as: "An economic strategy based on the use of measures (e.g. blockade) of which the primary effect is to weaken the economy of the other state."

On the 9th of May 1944, in the House of Lords, there was a debate on the subject of Economic Warfare during which Lord Selborne, Minister of Economic Warfare, contributed the following:

"By these means Germany has been prevented from using her Atlantic seaboard to import food and raw materials. When Japan entered the war at the end of 1941, our enemies tried to break the blockade, and it was very important for them to do so, because it so happened that their economies were complementary: Japan had tungsten, the rubber, and the oil that Germany so much needed; Germany had precision tools, blueprints, ball-bearings and the like, all of which Japan required very much. And therefore, they started a system of fast blockade runners that ran from the East to West and from West to East without showing lights or using their wireless or calling at any port.

For a time, they had limited success, but before long, the Royal Navy, the Navies of our Allies and the Air Forces were able to get on the job, and we have altogether sunk some fifteen blockade runners, four outward and eleven inward. Now that traffic, except for a few submarines, which can carry very little, has practically ceased. The cargoes that were destroyed included 45,000 tons of rubber, 1,500 tons of tungsten, 17,000 tons of tin, 25,000 tons of vegetable oils, and Far Eastern drugs of great importance, such as quinine. But it was not the cargoes that were sunk that were most important, it was the cargoes that never sailed on account of the way we were able to demonstrate that the blockade could be enforced." (Hansard)

Undoubtedly, intelligence gathering behind enemy lines contributed to the Allies knowing when a ship would sail and what its cargo would be.

Where the SOE's Economic Warfare in China was concerned, the biggest player, quite literally, was Walter Fletcher, a businessman weighing in at some nineteen stone who was always counted as two passengers when flying. "He made no secret of living on the borderline between honest merchanting and smuggling." (Foot, M.R.D)

Colin Mackenzie, the Head of Force 136 commented:

"Walter was gloriously fat. It was rumoured that he won the hundred yards at Charterhouse when he was nineteen stone. I didn't believe it but when I saw him running for a bus when he was still nineteen stone, I began to believe it."

Walter Fletcher's (1892–1956) CV covered businessman, WW1 veteran, SOE operative, smuggler, fine artist and Conservative politician. Born Walter Fleischl Von Marxow, the son of a naturalised Austrian Jew. He was said to have 'an unusually brilliant mind and an equally stimulating personality but, at times, difficult to get on with'. (National Archives)

After an education that began at Charterhouse School and then the University of Lausanne, his career began as a trainee manager in the rubber industry.

During WW1, he served in the Army Ordinance Department in East Africa where he was promoted to the rank of Major. In recognition of his service, he was mentioned in despatches and also received an OBE. (National Archives Blog.)

After the War, he went back to Africa to manage a number of rubber plantations and then returned to Britain where he became managing director of Hecht, Levis and Khan, a major rubber and commodities company.

In 1940, Fletcher approached the SOE and his knowledge and expertise saw him assigned to Force 136. In 1945, he was initially elected as Conservative MP for Bury and in 1950 following boundary changes, he was elected MP for Bury and Radcliffe. He was knighted in 1953.

At the outbreak of the Second World War, Fletcher had tried to enlist but he failed his medical. Determined to play a role in this conflict, Fletcher then tried to join the SOE but was initially unsuccessful because he was again deemed unfit to carry out tasks that involved any physical effort. By this time, he had come to the attention of Hugh Dalton who described him as 'a thug with good commercial contacts'. He was further described as having, 'an unusually brilliant mind and an equally stimulating personality but, at times, difficult to get on with'. (Berliner, P.)

Fletcher's first involvement in Economic Warfare was an attempt to buy the Dutch East Indies' rubber crop, and to smuggle rubber out of Malaysia and Indo-China, to prevent the Japanese getting their hands on it. He initially sought an advance of £500,000 from the British Government to cover any expenses, however, he only received £100,000. After two years, his efforts were closed down because he had failed to produce any rubber at all. However, he was a good businessman and so, two years later, he persuaded the Treasury and the SOE to allow him to switch his attention to China. Fletcher particularly wanted to run a mission that would enable the SOE to be able to manipulate the Chinese Black Market.

Smuggling was rife in China at this time as Stanfield witnessed:

"There is a terrific black market and as a consequence, plenty of smuggling. You would have been amused at customs in Calcutta, searching a Chinese general. They found gold rings, watches etc. all over him and wearing three suits. They only fined him 500 rupees, but he would make ten times that amount by selling a little of his stuff."

Chinese magnates and their wives and mistresses were ready to pay large sums for scarce goods such as diamonds, high end Swiss watches, medical drugs, indigo and cigarette paper. Undoubtedly, some of these Chinese magnates and their wives and mistresses would attend the Japanese surrender ceremony in Peking in October 1945, wearing their expensive watches and jewellery.

Fletcher was also involved in the purchase of silkworm eggs for the Kashmir silk industry to make parachute silk.

The diamonds were supplied by the South African Government, under Prime Minister General Smuts, from De Beers while the watches were purchased and then smuggled out through France by operatives who thought they were carrying gunsights for the RAF. Fletcher then sold them in an operation named 'Operation

Remorse', previously known as Operation Mickleham, at prices that were inflated because of the items' scarcity value and it was known as the, 'biggest currency black market in history'. (Cruikshank, C.) In the field Operation Remorse was run by four officers under the command of Lionel Davis, supported by Alexander Stewart (Remorse Accountant and representative of John Venner), Bernard Myles (Senior Remorse Accountant) and Edward Wharton-Tigar.

Due to the war, inflation was high in China and the official rate of exchange from Chinese Yuan to sterling was twenty-four to the pound while on the black market, it was more like four hundred to the pound.

> **De Beers Group is an international corporation that specializes in diamond mining, diamond exploitation, diamond retail, diamond trading and industrial diamond manufacturing sectors.**

The Operation raised some two billion pounds and the net profit of seventy-seven million pounds was then used to fund the SOE's activities worldwide.

The United States viewed China as one of its areas of operation and consequently, it was agreed, by treaty, that the SOE was not to operate there. Fletcher had a number of contacts in China and so he ignored the treaty, viewing his role as importantly making friends and influencing people rather than that of an operative who had to follow orders, but despite the success of Operation Remorse, the SOE became worried particularly as Fletcher was proving hard to control.

In April 1945, Operation Remorse became involved in a humane operation that came to be known as 'Operation Waldorf'. Thousands of French soldiers had fought their way from Indo-China to what they assumed was the relative safety of China's Yunnan Province. The United States were awkward about providing the French with ammunition to defend what was a French colonial possession, until Churchill reminded President Roosevelt that 'letting men die, merely to satisfy anti-imperial dogma, would look bad in the eyes of posterity'. The United States' assistance fell short of what was required while the Chinese also did very little apart from disarming the French soldiers. Therefore, Operation Remorse stepped in to avert a tragedy. It was a difficult task as the 5,500 French soldiers, needing food, medical supplies, blankets and clothing, were spread across eight locations. Financially, it was an expensive operation as the SOE had to, first of all, acquire what was needed and then transport 93 tons of supplies over a period of six weeks. Operation Waldorf was a success. (National Archives)

Operation Remorse was also involved in bribing officials which was both illegal and politically sensitive which seems strange given the nature of SOE's other operations. A reminder was circulated that 'although Remorse is a department of SOE, its activities are confined to financial and commodity matters only'. (National Archives). In response, Fletcher wrote to Lionel Davis stating that:

"Trading ventures will, in reality, be a smokescreen to transfer profits and bribes to those whom we take into partnership with the ultimate end of having Chinese provincial authorities, both military and civil, on our side." (National Archives)

Despite the above, in October 1945, the decision was made to take Fletcher out of Operation Remorse by promoting him to a post where he became responsible for special financial and economic operations and as a result, he was overseen by John Venner, SOE's Head of Finance. In October 1945, Venner told Fletcher that his employment with the SOE was ending citing the fact that Fletcher, 'as an MP and company chairman, he couldn't keep up his secretive pursuits'. Fletcher was unhappy about this, claiming that he had been 'treated in a very unsatisfactory manner'. (National Archives)

Operation Remorse itself was disbanded in November 1945, but not before it began a final operation in Hong Kong to restore confidence in British banking which was achieved by using Chinese National Dollars (CND) to buy Hong Kong dollars, plus getting favourable news items in the press. Within twelve days, the value of the Hong Kong dollar had increased from 80 to 140 CND.

5.   Chinese Nationalists

"The sky cannot have two suns."
(Chiang Kai-Shek)

The Chinese Nationalists believed that the Chinese people were a nation and looked to promote all cultures together with national unity of all the Chinese people. This was the polar opposite of the warlords reigning over their parts of China who saw themselves as superior to China's existing ethnicities. However, as the years passed, the words of the Nationalists did not match their actions pointing therefore, to a credibility issue.

The terms Chiang Kai-Shek and the Chinese Nationalists are synonymous and therefore you cannot speak or write about one without the other having to be included too. Chiang Kai-Shek attended a Military Academy in Japan 1907–11 and then 1909–1911, he served in the Japanese army. While in Tokyo, he joined a group of young Chinese men who were plotting to overthrow the Emperor and through them, Chiang Kai-Shek became a revolutionary and a republican. Following the civil war that broke out in 1911, Chiang Kai-Shek returned to China and took part in the fighting that led to the overthrow of Emperor Puyi.

Prince Puyi became Emperor of Japan in 1908 at the age of two years and ten months and at the age of six, he was forced to abdicate following the 1911 Revolution which saw the creation of the Republic of China. Emperor Puy's abdication saw the end of two thousand years of Imperial rule.

Emperor Puyi (1906–1967) came to the Imperial Throne in 1908 and abdicated in 1912. Puyi was allowed to continue living in the palace in Peking and he chose Henry as a given name and was known in the West as 'Henry Puyi'.

In July 1917, he was very briefly restored to the throne by a loyalist general, Zhang Xun, for a period of eleven days. In 1924, he was expelled from the Palace, and made his way to Tianjin where he began to put out feelers to the warlords on both sides of the civil conflict.

In 1932, the Japanese made him Emperor of Manchuko which he ruled until the end of the war with Japan in 1945. He was totally under the control of the Japanese and signed everything they put in front of him, including an edict making slavery legal.

In 1922, he had married Empress Wanrong and during their time isolated in the Salt Tax Palace, his wife became addicted to opium and as a result, they were distant towards each other. He also frequently ordered his servants to be beaten. In 1945, when it became clear that Japan was defeated, he fled his palace but was captured by the Russians who allowed him to be extradited to the People's Republic of China in 1949. After his capture, he never saw Empress Wanrong again and she died of starvation in a Chinese prison in 1946.

Puyi appeared before the Tokyo War Crimes Court and although the expectation was that he would be executed, he was imprisoned for war crimes for a period of ten years because Mao Tse-tung saw value in him becoming a re-educated commoner. After his re-education and while still in prison he wrote his memoirs with the 'help' of a ghost writer and on his release, he became a member of the Chinese People's Political Consultative Conference and the National People's Congress. His re-education led to him apologising for his actions and cruelty when he was Emperor.

In April 1962, he married Li Shuxian, a hospital nurse and then died in 1967. He was buried in what is described as a commercial cemetery.

Despite the overthrow of the Emperor, the fighting continued. Sun Yat-sen was elected as the first Provisional President of the Republic of China, however, he was in a weak position militarily. At Sun Yat-sen's request, Yuan Shikai arranged for the abdication of the child emperor Pu Yi in return for being granted the position of President of the Republic of China. Yuan Shikai was not present when the Abdication edict was issued, but with the situation getting worse for his party, Sun Yat-sen fled to Japan in August 1913.

China's republican/nationalist movement then had to take on China's first President, Yuan Shikai, who had ambitions to become the new Emperor. Seeing the situation for his party worsen and with Sun Yat-sen having fled to Japan, the Chinese Nationalists called for a Second Revolution, this time against Yuan Shikai. Yuan Shikai gradually took over the government, using the military as the basis of his power. He dissolved the national and provincial assemblies, and the House of Representatives and Senate were replaced by the newly formed 'Council of State', with Duan Qirui as Prime Minister.

In January 1914, Yuan Shikai dissolved China's Government and formed a new cabinet which, in May, produced a new constitution that replaced the provisional version. The new constitution gave Yuan Shikai unlimited powers over China's military, finances, foreign policy and the rights of the Chinese people, which he justified by stating that the county's democracy had not worked because of the political infighting.

In 1915, rumours started to spread that there was support for the reinstatement of the monarchy based on the argument that the country's political situation needed the stability that only a dynastic monarchy could provide. This reasoning is interesting because if the monarchy was so important why had it been overthrown just three years before?

From 1916–1918, Chiang Kai-shek absented himself from national politics and went to live in Shanghai. However, in 1918, he joined Sun Yatsen's Nationalist Party. Eventually, Sun Yat-sen returned from Japan and created a revolutionary government in the south to challenge the grip of the warlords. Chiang Kai-Shek's close relationship with Sun Yat-sen enabled him to start on his path to power. Following the death of Yuan Shikai, the Nationalists' priority was to reunify China, which was now in the hands of Chinese warlords.

> **Yuan Shikai (1859–1916) was both a Chinese military and government official who eventually became Emperor of the Empire of China from the 12th of December 1915 to the 22nd of March 1916. He tried to save the dynasty but at the same time to modernise it with**

projects covering the bureaucracy, education, fiscal reform, and the judiciary. He formed China's first modern army and a more efficient government in Northern China.

On the 22nd of March, after being emperor for only 83 days, he stepped down due to mounting opposition throughout the country and increasing ill health. He held on to the post of President, despite increasing opposition, until he died just three months later.

Like all leaders in China, he was an autocrat, relying on both the military and the bureaucracy for his power. Like all autocrats, when that support wanes, they have little choice but to stand down even if they lead a counter-revolt.

In 1922, Sun Yat-sen had signed an agreement with the Soviet representative, Adolf Joffe. This agreement highlighted Chinese unity, both Nationalists and Communists, and the Comintern (representing the Communist International based in Moscow). The Nationalists under Sun Yat-sen had grown closer to the Soviet Union when the Western Allies had refused to help him defeat the warlords in the North. Sun Yat-sen reorganised the Nationalist Party along Soviet lines, and so, Chiang Kai-Shek, at that moment, a young lieutenant, was sent to the Soviet Union in 1923 to study Soviet institutions, especially the Red Army. Back in China after four months, he became commandant of a military academy, which was based on the Soviet model, at Whampoa.

Adolf Joffe (1883–1927) was a communist revolutionary, diplomat and politician who was closely aligned with Leon Trotsky and the two of them co-edited the newspaper, Pravda.

Joffe was elected to the Bolshevik Central Committee in August 1917 and supported Lenin when he sought the socialist revolution in October 1917 and became Chairman of the Petrograd Military Revolutionary Committee.

When Russia sought a treaty with the Germans, Joffe headed the delegation that went to Brest-Litovsk. Still very much a supporter of Trotsky, he opposed the signing of the Treaty; however, it was eventually signed. Joffe paid for his opposition by being sidelined from party leadership roles in 1919 and instead, he was given overseas diplomatic missions including China in the early 1920s where he arranged help for the Chinese Nationalists.

Joffe's support for Trotsky made him anxious for his own safety when Trotsky was expelled from the Communist Party, on top of which he was suffering severe health issues, and so he committed suicide in November 1927.

Sun Yat-sen's admiration of the Soviet Union led to Soviet advisers arriving in China, and as a result of the 1922 agreement, Chinese communists were allowed into the Nationalist Party. After Sun Yat-sen's death in 1925, the leadership of the Nationalists passed to Wang Jingwei, while Chiang Kai-Shek, who by 1926, was Chief of Staff of the Kuomintang's National Revolutionary Army (NRA) and also had the support of a number of secret societies in China, the army and the Soviets. At the same time, the Chinese communists were growing stronger under the leadership of Mao Tse-tung which inevitably led to tensions between the two parties who set about destabilising the country through rent strikes, worker uprisings and anti-landlord rallies.

Wang Jingwei (1883–1944), was a Chinese politician. At first, he was a member of the left wing of the Kuomintang and progressed to being the leader of the Nationalist government in Wuhan which was in direct opposition to the right-wing, military government in Nanjing led by Chiang Kai-Shek. Later, he became increasingly anti-communist after his efforts to collaborate with the Chinese Communist Party ended in political failure.

The NRA was, at that time, the largest army in the world having some four million men spread across 346 Divisions. However, very few of them had received military training or weapons, all meals consisted of rice and there was one blanket between five soldiers. (Donovan, 2004). In addition, many of the divisions were commanded by warlords who acted on the basis that their men would obey them and not Chiang Kai-Shek. It might have been the largest army in the world, but it was not all-conquering due to a lack of military discipline, weapons and supplies and therefore, it is a reasonable to ask the question why? The answer was Chiang Kai-Shek who withheld weapons and equipment from all but those he trusted, therefore, they were to be no match for the disciplined Japanese Army.

The NRA then moved north to defeat the warlords achieving success in the early stages of this conflict and leading to the absorption of some of the Warlords' armies thereby doubling its troops to some 250,000. The success of the NRA enabled Chiang Kai-Shek, when Nanking had been retaken, to set up a rival military government, effectively a military dictatorship, to the civilian one under Wang Jingwei that was based in Wuhan.

Meanwhile, the Chinese Communists were based in Shanghai by 1927. Initially, Chiang Kai-Shek chose to keep the Communists off-balance by switching between shows of force and leniency. The trick he had to pull off, though, was to stop the Communists' growing influence without losing Soviet support.

As the NRA advanced on Shanghai, the Communists overthrew the local warlord which made Chiang Kai-Shek even more determined to overthrow them. When the NRA had taken Shanghai, Chiang Kai-Shek closed the city's temporary municipal government set up by the Communists and then three days later, he declared martial law. After a further three days, the Chinese Nationalists began to massacre Chinese Communists and other left wing party members in Shanghai killing an estimated 4,000 people. The massacre served to firstly boost the influence of the Communists in rural areas under the leadership of Mao Tse-Tung which secondly, forced the leadership of the Communist Party to review its revolutionary strategy (see next chapter).

Moscow had supported the Nationalists until 1927, when Chiang Kai-Shek finally broke with the Communists, expelling them from the Nationalist Party and suppressing the labour unions they had organised. Moscow now aligned itself solely with the Chinese Communists. Shortly afterwards, Wang Jingwei's government in Wuhan collapsed leaving Chiang Kai-Shek in overall control of the Chinese Nationalists.

As Chiang Kai-Shek had prioritised the defeat of the Communists, this gave the Japanese a free hand to then exploit the civil war. As a result, the Japanese then invaded Manchuria in September 1931 on the pretext that the Chinese Nationalists had destroyed a Japanese railway in the city of Mukden, although the real reason was the economic problems created by the United States. Japan saw Manchuria as its lifeline and believed it should have exclusive rights over the Chinese mainland. This was followed by the installation of Puyi as the puppet monarch of Manchukuo (country of the Manchus) which would receive Japanese support. The Japanese wanted and would eventually seek to take control of Northern China. This led Chiang Kai-Shek to have to rethink his strategy.

The Nationalists retook Peking and then moved south to create a new capital in Nanking. With the Japanese steadily advancing, Chiang Kai-Skek had no option but to recognise that in order to defeat them, the two sides, Nationalist and Communist, had to put aside their differences and work together.

> **Chiang Kai-Shek (1887–1975) was a Chinese Nationalist politician, revolutionary and military leader who served as the leader of the Republic of China between 1928 and 1975, first in mainland China until 1949 and then in Taiwan until his death.**

The Japanese attack on Manchuria caused concern in both London and Washington about Japanese aggression in South-East Asia. However, their concern wasn't sufficient for them to do anything about it despite China being allied to the United States. In the late nineteenth century, the United States formed an alliance with China in the hope that China would balance Japanese influence in the Pacific. There was, though, a second objective of this alliance for the United States, namely that China would provide a market for United States exportable surpluses, but this would need China to stay solvent and out of the hands of the Japanese.

As a result, and desperate for support, Chiang Kai-Shek appealed to the United Nations. The phrase: 'United Nations' was first used by the American President Roosevelt in the 'Declaration by United Nations' on the 1st of January 1942 when representatives of 26 nations came together to pledge their governments to continue fighting together against the Axis Powers (Appendix 5). The United Nations as the world knows it now did not exist until the 24th of October 1945 and so Chiang Kai-Shek's appeals therefore were to the unofficial United Nations which condemned Japanese aggression but took no further action.

When Japan eventually invaded China in 1937, it was not, strangely, the official start of a war that was to last until 1945, and therefore, the Japanese's Shanghai Campaign and the Nanking Massacre were not officially acts of war.

On the 11th of January 1938, an Imperial Conference was held in Tokyo which was attended by Emperor Hirohito. Prime Minister Konoye presented the Conference with what he called a 'Fundamental Policy' to deal with China. The policy was in fact an ultimatum to the Chinese Nationalist Government. It contained severe terms, including the payment of reparations to Japan, and new political arrangements to formally recognise the separation of North China which would remain under Japanese control. Chiang Kai-Shek and his government were given 72 hours to accept the Japanese demands and if they refused, then Japan would no longer recognise the Chinese Government and in fact, would destroy it.

By the 16th of January, the Chinese Government had not yet responded and so the China-Japanese war officially started with the Japanese boasting that they could capture Shanghai in three days and the whole of China in three months.

Another key figure in the push for war against China was General Tojo who had progressed through the officer ranks because of his attention to detail. He was also supported by a Japanese Army faction which had been formed to seek upgrades to Japan's fighting capabilities in a time of tight budgets and what it saw as civilian interference. Tojo had served as head of the Japanese Military Police in Manchuria and after he became the Army's Chief of Staff in 1937; he had a significant role in opening hostilities against China. Tojo quickly became certain that the only way to get the Chinese Government to work with Japan was to occupy Chinese territory. He returned to Japan in 1938 and took up the post of Army Vice-Minister and became Army Minister in 1940 and all the time he was advocating increasing the level of conflict with China.

Tojo also saw benefits for Japan entering into an alliance with Germany and Italy and this happened in September 1940 with the signing of a Tripartite Pact by Germany's Foreign Minister, Von Ribbentrop, Italy's Foreign Minister, Galeazzo Ciano, 2nd Count of Cortellazzo and Buccari, and the Japanese Ambassador, Saburo Kuruso in Berlin (Appendix 4). The pact, known as the 'Pact of Steel', allowed for mutual assistance in the event of one of signatories being attacked by a nation not already involved in the war. The main objective of the pact, where Germany and Italy were concerned, was to dissuade the United States from entering the war.

In the build-up to the signing, a secret meeting was held in Tokyo, in the presence of Emperor Hirohito, to discuss the forthcoming pact. Japan wanted the pact to give it a freehand in South-East Asia which was acceptable to Germany knowing that it would drain military resources away from the European conflict.

Emperor Hirohito finally approved the document on the 13th of September because he knew what was being planned, namely an attack on Pearl Harbour which would inevitably lead to war with the United States. This war was in response to the United States in 1941 deciding to introduce a complete embargo on oil and steel exports to Japan. For Japan, this meant finding alternative markets and it therefore created, 'The Greater East Asia Co-Prosperity Sphere' the sub-text to which was a plan to colonise the South-East Asian countries and thereby secure supplies of oil and steel.

On the 2nd of December 1941, Japan urged Germany to join it in declaring war on the United States. Japan had only informed Germany of its intention to go to war just two days before. This demonstrated a level of naivety on the part of the Japanese Government because Germany was not interested in fighting in South-East Asia. The German Government was more interested in seeing the Western Allies forced into opening up another front, thereby diverting troops and resources. The German Government did not respond and so Japan approached Italy which in turn led to a joint declaration of war on the 11th of December against the United States by Germany and Italy and an agreement, that neither Germany, Italy, or Japan would make a separate peace with the United States. The articles of the agreement were:

ARTICLE I: Italy, Germany and Japan will henceforth conduct in common and jointly a war which has been imposed on them by the United States of America and England, by all means at their disposal and until the end of hostilities.

ARTICLE II: Italy, Germany and Japan undertake each for himself that none of the parties to the present accord will conclude either armistice or peace, be it with the United States or with England without complete and reciprocal agreement [of the three signatories to this pact].

ARTICLE III: Italy, Germany and Japan, even after the victorious conclusion of this war, will collaborate closely in the spirit of the Tripartite Pact, concluded on the 21st of Sept. 1940, in order to realise and establish an equitable new order in the world.

ARTICLE IV: The present accord is effective immediately on its signature and remains in force for the duration of the Tripartite Pact, signed 27 Sept. 1940. The high contracting parties of this accord will, at an opportune moment, agree among themselves the means of implementing Article III above of this accord.

*****

On the 16th of September, President Roosevelt and Prime Minister Churchill were at the Second Quebec Conference. The conference was mainly focused on the war in Europe, but they still found time to discuss Stilwell's complaint that Chiang Kai-Shek was refusing to provide relief for the troops in Burma. There was little support and reinforcements to help the Chinese, Indian, Nepalese Gurkhas and the British and American forces, however, what was really needed was a leader with vision, determination, creativity and the ability to manage Chiang Kai-Shek. Roosevelt was worried that Burma was heading for disaster and his reply insisted that Chiang Kai-Shek should be ordered not to withdraw his men from Burma but, also, should send more men to bolster those already there.

In the note sent by Roosevelt to Chiang Kai-Shek, he wrote that he would have to bear responsibility if the land route between China and Burma was cut. The sting in the tail was that Roosevelt wrote that General Stilwell would assume command over the Chinese forces. To add salt to the wound, Stilwell insisted on delivering the note to Chiang Kai-Shek himself. Roosevelt's note was to sour relations between China and the United States for many years to come.

6. Chinese Communists

"The enemy advances, we retreat. The enemy halts and encamps, we harass.
The enemy seeks to avoid battle, we attack. The enemy retreats, we pursue."

(The Communists military principles summed up in four maxims by Mao Tse-
Tung and Zhu De)

Mao Tse-Tung did not have a poor upbringing. His father had been a poor
peasant and a former soldier, but he had become a grain merchant with two and
a half acres of land. Mao's father was bad tempered and when Mao realised that
nothing he did would reduce his father's anger, he became a rebellious young
man. Mao had little time for teachers and for the rest of his life, he chose to
ignore them.

> **Mao Tse-Tung (1893–1976) entered a teacher-training college in
> 1913 in Changsha where he formed a number of student
> organisations. Having qualified in 1918, he moved to Peking where he
> became an assistant in the university library.**
>
> **It was then that he fell under the influence of two founding
> members of the Marxists and founders of the Chinese Communist
> Party, Dr Li-Dazhao and Chen Duxiu.**
>
> **Mao returned to Changsha in 1920 where he became principal of
> a primary school and started to form Changsha's branch of the
> Chinese Communist Party. By 1921, he was General Secretary of
> Huna's Communist Party and was one of the twelve delegates who
> attended to First Party Congress at a time when the national
> membership of the Party was just sixty.**
>
> **In 1949, having defeated the Japanese and driven out the Chinese
> Nationalists, the Chinese Communist Party came to power and over
> which he ruled until his death in 1976.**

In 1927, the Chinese Communist Party (CCP) had seized power in Shanghai in anticipation of the man it saw as its liberator, General Chiang Kai-Shek. This turned out to be a near fatal mistake that almost led to the demise of the Chinese Communist Party as Chiang Kai-Shek set out to destroy what he saw as a threat to his regime, the CCP.

Mao's followers retreated to Ya'an Province and on arrival, they joined up with Zhu De and his followers. The march had taken its toll and fewer than one in ten of his followers survived. Zhu De and his followers joined forces with those of Mao and although weakened by Chiang Kai-Shek's onslaught, it was the birth of the Red Army.

Zhu De (1886–1976) was a Chinese general, warlord, politician and revolutionary of the Chinese Communist Party. In 1911, he graduated from the Yunnan Military Academy after which he served as an officer in the armies of warlords in Sichuan and Yunnan Provinces. By 1922, he was frustrated by the situation in China and left the country to travel to the University of Gottingen in Germany. Later he moved on to Berlin where he joined the Chinese Communist Party, and later was forced to leave due to his political activities.

He then travelled to the Soviet Union to study military affairs and Marxism before returning to China in 1926. Hiding his membership of the Chinese Communist Party, he then became an officer in the Nationalist Army in August 1927, saw him take part in the Communist led uprising in Nanchang which is seen by the Communists as the birth of the Red Army. The Nationalists crushed the uprising and Zhu led the remaining troops south, eventually linking up with Mao's guerilla forces and establishing a base in Jiangxi Province. During the journey south, Zhu De's wife was captured and executed with her head stuck on a pole in Changsa.

Zhu was to be the military commander and Mao the political commissar. Zhu's Red Army numbered 5,000 in 1929 rising to 200,000 in 1933.

Zhu successfully commanded the Red Army's defence against the first four offensives between 1931–33. After the fifth offensive proved successful, the Red Army made its way north, the Long March, and when the Communists and the Nationalists formed an alliance against

the Japanese in 1937, Zhu commanded the Red Army's forces in the north and eventually nationally until the Japanese surrender in 1945. During the civil war that followed, he commanded the People's Liberation Army until the Nationalists were defeated in 1949 and continued as its commander until 1954. His tactics were based on large scale guerilla war as per the military principles as set out below. He was made a Marshall in 1955 and from 1959 he was Chairman of the Standing Committee of the National People's Congress.

By that time, the Party membership had shrunk from some 300,000 to just 40,000 leaving the Party looking finished. In its weakened state, the Communists had to survive five offensives from the Nationalists whose objective was to capture the Communist enclave. The Communists managed to repel the Nationalists through a combination of mobile infiltration and guerilla tactics based on their military principles that were summed up in the following:

1. The enemy advances, we retreat.
2. The enemy halts and encamps, we harass.
3. The enemy seeks to avoid battle, we attack.
4. The enemy retreats, we pursue.

For the fifth offensive, Chiang Kai-Shek assembled some 700,000 men and established a number of cement blockhouses around the perimeter of the Red Army's position. In early 1934, the CCP removed Mao as its leader replacing him with Zhu De as its military commander and Chou En-Lai as its political commissar.

Chou En-Lai (1898–1976) was an important figure in the Chinese Communist Party rising to the posts of Foreign Minister (1949–1958) and Prime Minister (1946–76). He had been a member of the Chinese Communists since 1921.

He was renowned for his negotiating skills and eye for details, and he was seen as a man who was affable, charming, pragmatic and persuasive traits that helped him to survive amongst the internal rivalries in the party.

On 14 Feb. 1950, Zhou signed in Moscow a 30–year Chinese-Soviet treaty of alliance, and, at the 1955 Afro-Asian conference, that convened at Bandung, where he offered China's support to Asian non-aligned nations. In 1956, he was elected one of the party's four vice chairmen. Following the Cultural Revolution, (1966–1976) he remained the third ranking member of the Standing Committee of the Politburo During the Cultural Revolution, his personality traits were evident in the way he calmed things down in what was a chaotic period.

During the waning of the Cultural Revolution in the early 1970s, Zhou sought to restore Deng Xiaoping and other former moderate leaders to positions of power.

(Based on the Editors of Encyclopedia Britannica – the 1st of March 2021)

Zhu De's first action was to abandon Mao's military tactics and replaced them with a more positional form of warfare which was conducted along permanent and fortified front lines as was the case in the First World War. Up to the First World War, warfare was more mobile and tended to depend heavily on cavalry. This change subsequently proved to be a disaster.

The Red Army was pushed back, suffering heavy losses. In October 1934, surrounded by the Nationalists, 86,000 Communists managed to break out and led by Mao; the 1st Army fled west with no particular destination in mind. This was to become known as the Long March when during the first three months, he was to lose half his army due to constant ground and air attacks. The women on the march feared pregnancy more than anything else the march might burden them with. The fear was that when a baby cried, it could alert enemy forces and so if babies could not be given to either relatives or peasant families, they were abandoned; something that Mao's wife had to do on three occasions.

The Long March lasted 368 days, mainly moving at night, and according to the Communists official narrative, the journey covered 6,000 miles, crossed 18 mountains and 24 rivers although the length of the journey is disputed with some saying it was no more than 3,500 miles The length of the journey and the time it took enabled Mao to regain control of the Communist Party and the creation of a new base in North West China close to the Soviet border.

In January 1935, at an emergency meeting in Zunyi, Guizhou Province, Mao defeated the Party's pro-Moscow faction enabling him to regain the leadership of the Communist Party and in March 1935, Mao led his party north to the Soviet border under continuing attacks from the Nationalists and Muslim and Tibetan warlords. As the march continued, the 1st Army came into contact with the 4th Army under the command of Zhang Guotao in the Sichuan–Shaanxi border area which inevitably led to another power struggle which saw Zhang's men march south.

Mao and the 1st Army continued to march north to join up with the Communist leaders Gao Gang and Liu Zhidan who had established a new base at Shaanxi. By the time Mao arrived, the 1st Army numbered 8,000, and they merged with the local Red Army force which numbered 7,000. Eventually, the 2nd and 4th Armies arrived bringing the total up to 30,000 at which point the Long March was over.

> **Gao Gang (1905–1954) was a Communist Party of China leader during the Chinese Civil War and the early years of the People's Republic of China before becoming the victim of the first major purge within the CPC since before 1949. In 1952, he was ordered to Beijing to become Head of the State Planning Commission of China. Later he attempted a leadership challenge against Liu Shaoqi and Zhou Enlai. His attempt failed and he committed suicide in August 1954.**
>
> **Liu Zhidan (1902–1936) as a Chinese military commander and Communist leader, who founded the Shaanxi-Gansu-Ningxia Base Area in northwest China, which became the Yan'an Soviet, the primary base of the Chinese Communists until 1947**
>
> **In 1935, the Nationalist army attacked Liu's base but were beaten in the Battle of Laoshan. Liu then fell victim to a vicious purge and he and many of his comrades were jailed and Liu was sentenced to death. He was saved by the arrival of Mao and his Long Marchers who promptly put a stop to what was going on. Liu was killed in battle in February 1936.**

Despite the Japanese invasion, Chiang Kai-Skek still wanted to continue the civil war. As a result, he ordered the Nationalist's NE Army under General Zhang Xueliang and the 17th Army under General Yang Hucheng to attack Mao's forces in the Shaanxi area. On the 12th of December 1936, Chiang Kai-Shek paid a visit to General Zhang's headquarters in Xi'an to review the anti-communist campaign. Much to his surprise, Chiang Kai-Shek was arrested by General Zhang's troops while those accompanying him were arrested by troops of General Yang's 17th Army. While Chiang Kai-Shek and his party remained under arrest, negotiations started to forge an alliance with the Communists to resist the Japanese. The negotiations were successfully concluded and on the 26th of December, Chiang Kai-Shek verbally agreed with his two generals' proposals and so the civil war was put on hold.

By December 1936, the Party was once more united and Ya'nan became the Communist Party's base until 1945. Having a base enabled the Red Army to be trained and indoctrinated at the Resist Japan University.

January 1941 saw the 'New Fourth Army Incident' and both sides put their own interpretation on events. Mao had agreed to withdraw his forces to the Yangtse River but that did not stop the Nationalists attacking them for what it claimed was insubordination. The incident followed an unsuccessful Communist, all-out offensive against the Japanese Army. The Communists felt that the Red Army was sufficiently strong enough to launch an attack on Japanese-held cities and railway lines. All the Red Army succeeded in doing was destroying 600 miles of rail track and causing the temporary closure of the important Jingxi coalmine.

The Japanese Army was not as weak as the Communists had thought and launched a counter-attack. The fighting ended in January 1941 with the Communists contained and suffering heavy losses. The Japanese Army was urged by its commander to adopt what was referred to as the 'three alls' policy, namely, *Kill all, burn all, loot all*. The Communists learnt a hard lesson resulting in the Red Army returning to guerilla warfare.

The two-hour Japanese attack on the US Naval base at Pearl Harbour on the 7th of December 1941, left 2,400 Americans dead, twenty-one ships either sunk of damaged, and around 188 US aircraft destroyed. As a result, China became an important ally of the United States, its importance being that it would tie down thousands of Japanese troops.

To help China, the United States sent General Stilwell to become Chief of Staff to Chiang Kai-Shek, formulated a lend-lease agreement that provided five billion dollars over the period 1941–46. Unfortunately, the relationship between Stilwell and Chiang Kai-Shek was not good based on the corruption that he saw, the Nationalists repression of those that they governed and most importantly, he disagreed with Chiang Kai-Shek's policy of wearing down the Japanese. It was thanks to Chiang Kai-Shek's wife, Soong Meiling, who had a better relationship with the Americans, thereby securing the aid that the Nationalists required. However, getting supplies into China was difficult, as the key land routes through Burma and Vietnam were inaccessible thanks to the Japanese, so supplies had to be flown in over the Himalayas. The Russians too found supplying the Chinese difficult through Xinjiang Province as the local warlord was anti-Soviet.

Chiang Kai-Shek's forces demonstrated its value following the fall of Hong Kong when it defeated the Japanese Army at Changsha in South-East China. The Chinese Nationalist forces also fought in Burma from 1942–43, in cooperation with British and Commonwealth forces. In 1943, they repelled Japanese offensives in Hubei and Changde. The Japanese Ichi-Go offensive, which started in April 1944, led the United States to lose confidence in Chiang Kai-Shek.

In July 1944, with the inevitable defeat of the Japanese now becoming clearer, the United States Army Observation Group attempted to form a relationship with Mao and the Communists travelling to Yan'an to meet Mao and came to the conclusion that unlike the Nationalists, the Communists enjoyed support across the country due to their competence and lack of corruption. The Group concluded that Mao would not, once in power, adopt a violent or radical path. A postscript to this is that senior members of the group would have serious questions to answer when the anti-Communist McCarthy era took hold in the United States.

By 1945, the Japanese had been defeated, with the help of the CCP and the formal surrender took place on the 21st of August 1945 at the Zhijang Airfield in Hunan Province. At the ceremony, Major General Takeo Imai handed over a map that revealed the positions across the country of around one million Japanese troops.

> **Major General Takeo Imai (1898–1982) was an officer in the Japanese Army and from 1944–45, he was Vice-Chief of the General Staff of the China Expeditionary Army. In 1945, he met with Chinese Army officers at Chichiang to negotiate the terms of surrender.**

Manchuria remained a strategically important part of China 'with its large reserves of iron ore and coal, its steel industry, and its dense forests and rich farmland'. (Farrell, T. Military History Monthly, December 2016). Stalin ordered Mao to move his forces towards Manchuria and as a result, the Soviets were able to hand over some 700,000 rifles, 18,000 machine guns, 4,000 artillery pieces and 860 aircraft.

On the way to Manchuria, Mao's forces were joined by demobilised troops, bandit fighters and men from the puppet Manchuko Army created by the Japanese.

Chiang had a good idea what the Soviets and the Chinese Communists were about, but his main objective was not to upset Stalin but nevertheless, he ordered General Du Yuming to reclaim Manchuria. The Soviet controlled ports of Dalian and Port Arthur refused permission for General Du Yuming's forces to disembark so they moved south and disembarked and having done so, they were able to use the railway to move 300 kilometres.

General Du Yuming (1904–1981) was a Chinese Nationalist field commander taking part in the Nationalists northern expedition into Manchurai. He had also taken part in campaigns in southern China and in Burma.

After the Japanese surrender in 1945, he was an important commander under Chiang Kai-Shek in the Chinese Civil War. He was captured in 1949, after the Battle of Huaihai, when the Communists launched a major offensive against the Nationalist Headquarters in Xuzhou in 1948. He served ten years as a prisoner of war.

After his release, he served in the Communist Government and was a member of the National Committee, People's Political Consultative Conference (1964–1978), and the Standing Committee of the People's Political Consultative Conference (1978–1981).

The comparison between General Du Yuming's forces and those of the Communist commander, Lin Biao, is interesting. The Communist forces had no experience of trench warfare and Lin Biao had himself only taken part in one ambush in 1937 whereas General Du Yuming had commanded Nationalist soldiers in major battles against the Japanese. The Nationalist soldiers, therefore, were well-trained and battle-ready, whereas the Communist soldiers were badly trained, poorly motivated and just wanted peace. The Communist soldiers sang a song *Defeat Japan so we can go home*;however, after the Japanese defeat, it was banned.

> **Lin Biao (1907–1971) was a Marshall of the People's Republic of China who was key to the Communist victory in the Chinese Civil War, especially in North-East China. Lin was the general who commanded the decisive Liaoshen and Pingjin Campaigns, in which he co-led the Manchurian Field Army to victory and led the People's Liberation Army into Beijing.**
>
> **Lin was behind the creation of the Little Red Book which contained a collection of Mao's very short quotations in 1958 as a means of developing the cult of Mao's personality.**
>
> **In 1955, he became a member of the Central Committee's thirteen-member Political Bureau and then in May 1958, he became a member of the Political Bureau's seven member Standing Committee.**
>
> **Lin played a prominent role in the first several years of the Cultural Revolution (1966–76), but in 1971, he allegedly sought to remove Chinese leader Mao and seize power; his plot was discovered, and he died under obscure circumstances. The Chinese government later announced that Lin was killed on the 13th of Sept. 1971, in an airplane crash in Mongolia as he was fleeing to the Soviet Union after having plotted unsuccessfully to assassinate Mao.**

With the Nationalist Army making inroads into Manchuria, Stalin concluded that the Communists stood little or no chance of victory, so in November 1945, he ordered Mao to retreat from the cities.

However, with the Japanese defeated, the Soviet forces left China in June 1946 and the civil war erupted again with no other distractions.

*****

6. British Army Aid National Archives

A paramilitary military organisation for British and Allied forces in Southern China.

Japan had invaded China in 1937, but it was only after the Japanese had bombed Pearl Harbour that China joined the Allies in their fight against Japan. In December 1941, the British Crown Colony of Hong Kong was surrendered to the Japanese after eighteen days of fighting. This led to the British garrison of some 10,000 men being placed in prisoner of war camps.

Professor Lindsay Ride was appointed professor of physiology in 1928 at the University of Hong Kong. He was later commissioned into the Hong Kong Volunteer Defence Corps and aware of the approaching Japanese Army; he sent his family to Australia. By 1941, he was the commander of the Hong Kong Field Ambulance Service. The Japanese took Hong Kong on Christmas Day 1941, and Ride, like many thousands of others, became a prisoner of war and was held in the prison at Sham Shui Po Barracks. With assistance from the Hong Kong guerilla forces, Ride managed to escape in January 1942 and made his way to Chungkin. While attached as a colonel to the Indian Army, Ride formed and commanded the BAAG.

Having failed to get the Japanese Army to supply adequate food and medical supplies for the camps, Colonel 'Doc' Ride decided to escape in an effort to inform the outside world what was happening in the camps and to try to get help that way.

Colonel Lindsay 'Doc' Ride (1898–1977) was an Australian physiologist, soldier and eventually, Vice Chancellor of Hong Kong University. He had sent his family back to Australia in anticipation of the Japanese invasion of Hong Kong when at the time he commanded the Hong Kong Field Ambulance Service. In 1942, he was appointed OBE and then CBE in 1944, a reward for his outstanding leadership. After the war, he received a knighthood.

Colonel Ride found two friends who were willing to help him. One was Lieutenant Molly and the other was Adjutant Lieutenant Davis. Ride also knew that he needed someone who could speak Cantonese. Li Yubi, who had been Ride's assistant at Hong Kong University and a soldier in the guard during the war, agreed to take on this role. They escaped from Sham Shui Po prisoner of war camp, subsequently making their way to China where Colonel Ride went on to form the British Army Aid Group (BAAG).

The BAAG, which became a military intelligence unit operating in South China, operated under the cover that it was a humanitarian aid organisation concerned with famine relief and medical aid. The BAAG was also a military escape and evasion organisation in China from 1942 to 1945, working first from Kukong and after August 1943, from Kweilin. The BAAG was part of MI9, reporting on military, political and economic conditions in both Hong Kong and China, to the Directorate of Military Intelligence General Headquarters in New Delhi. Its officers were mainly Europeans with a Hong Kong connection while the operatives were mainly local Hong Kong men and women.

> **MI9, the Military Intelligence department, responsible for support to resistance movements and POW escapes.**

The Kweilin headquarters were evacuated before the Japanese advanced in 1944 and operations were then organised from Kunming. After the Japanese surrender, BAAG moved to Hong Kong where it was disbanded on 31 December 1945.

The British Army Aid Group (BAAG) appeared in the British Army's order of battle as an M19 unit with the objective of helping prisoners of war and other internees escape from Japanese prisoner of war camps, however, it was also a military intelligence unit. Its officers were mainly European men, usually with a Hong Kong connection while its operatives, both men and women, tended to be local Hong Kong people who joined up to fight for the restoration of their homeland and freedom.

As well as the major objectives detailed above, its operatives also conveyed news to their anxious families and friends and carried out scorched earth activities when the Japanese invaded interior bases. Many of these operatives were caught and suffered torture and death at the hands of the Japanese. The

BAAG operated in China from March 1942 until December 1945 and one important role was the provision of weather reports to the China Air Task Force of the United States Army Air Forces, who reciprocated by dropping medical supplies into the camps during raids.

In 1949, the Royal Hong Kong Defence Force was formed and Ride was appointed its commandant with the rank of colonel, rising to brigadier in 1956. Brigadier Ride retired in 1967.

*****

Major John Stanfield was posted to the BAAG and his cover was that he was a Signals Officer. A Signals Officer had a V2 wireless set which had six cell batteries and a major problem was keeping it charged as not many places enjoyed mains electricity. The answer was to charge it by hand which was a hard physical task.

Colonel Ride and the other escapees were helped by Hong Kong guerilla forces and managed to escape to Chunking, which the Japanese did not occupy at that time. The BAAG had its headquarters in Kwellin from where it supplied medical aid to the Chinese civilian population, many of whom had suffered in a variety of ways at the hands of the Japanese Army. When the Japanese had captured Kwellin, it was set on fire as part of their scorched earth policy.

As the Japanese advanced as part of Operation Ichi-go, BAAG found itself in the way and therefore had to leave the city in 'decrepit Bedford trucks on mud and stone roads, depending on wood alcohol, as petrol was unavailable except for the US Airforce'. (Major Stanfield) BAAG then sited its headquarters at Yi Shan where Major Stanfield's wireless station was 'an old graveyard'. The main activities that BAAG engaged in attempting to slow the Japanese advance by blowing up bridges and roads while the American Airforce bombed the Japanese airfields.

8. Japanese Army Atrocities

"Do not live in shame as a prisoner. Die and leave no ignominious crime behind you."
(From the Field Service Code issued by General Tojo in 1941.)

Japan is a marvelous place to visit for a holiday. The people are polite and the countryside, temples and cities are amazing. The Japanese people are honest to the extent that if you leave your purse or wallet on a shop counter, it will still be there when you go back. A relative and his partner who lived and worked in Japan, decided to go camping one weekend and while packing up their car, they put their tent on the pavement where it remained when they drove off. They were only going to be away for one night, so when they discovered their tent was missing, they decided to sleep in their car. The following day, they returned home and their tent was still where they left it. Would that happen in other countries?

However, modern Japan has proved very difficult to get to admit responsibility for the atrocities its troops engaged in and thereby to acknowledge its liability for compensation.

*****

There are many Hollywood films about the Japanese Army in World War Two that show a different side such as *Merry Christmas Mr Lawrence*, starring David Bowie, *The Bridge on the River Kwai* with Alec Guinness, and *Unbroken* starring Jack O'Connell, to name but three. Central to these films, is the cruelty meted out to Allied prisoners of war but this is also there in other Hollywood films and television series about the Japanese army – bayoneting patients and staff in hospitals being a prime example.

The China–Japan war is believed to have started on the 7th of July 1937 at the Marco Polo Bridge which led to the Japanese seizing the port city of Tianjin and then Peking. Later the city of Nanking was taken, resulting in Japanese atrocities that became known as the Nanking Massacre and the Rape of Nanking.

These and similar atrocities brought the United States into the picture and its efforts to help the Chinese was one of the reasons that led to the Japanese attack on Pearl Harbour and America formally entering the conflict.

The Nanking Massacre lasted from December 1937 until January 1938. The Chinese Nationalist Army had retreated from Nanking by the middle of December. The Japanese troops who entered the city were left by their officers to rape, pillage and plunder as they wanted. What followed was hideous – mass rapes and murders, thefts, and arson. China's official number of those killed is 300,000 while the Japanese claim the true figure is 30,000.

What was it about the Japanese officer class? Two Japanese officers, Toshiaki Mikai and Tsyuoshi Noda, indulged in a private contest to see who would be the first to murder one hundred Chinese using only their swords. Eventually that figure was met but being unable to say who had met the target first, they extended it to one hundred and fifty. Both officers survived the war but they were tried for war crimes and subsequently executed.

A paper by David Powers, *Japan: No Surrender in World War Two*, gives an explanation of the reasons behind these atrocities. Powers makes it clear that even in the face of insuperable odds, Japanese soldiers did not surrender. In fact, in the Field Service Code, issued by General Tojo in 1941, it is stated quite clearly that: 'Do not live in shame as a prisoner. Die, and leave no ignominious crime behind you'.

The BBC News website carried a story on the 14th of February 2021, by Anbarasan Ethirajan, under the headline *Kohima: Britain's 'forgotten' battle that changed the course of WWII*. This battle was fought in the North-East of India in May 1944. Fighting alongside the British were 'thousands of people from the Naga ethnic community', and only about a dozen are still alive today.

One of them is Sosangtemba Ao and he worked alongside the British for two months for one rupee per day. To this day, he still admires the fighting ability of the Japanese soldiers: "The Japanese army was highly motivated. Their soldiers did not fear death. For them, fighting for the emperor was divine. When they were asked to surrender, they would become suicide attackers."

Indeed, it was quite common for Japanese soldiers to include in letters home to their families photographs of people being beheaded or bayoneted by the Japanese.

General Tojo Hideki (1884–1948) was a soldier and was the Japanese Prime Minister from 1941–44. In the autumn of 1941, desperate talks were underway between the United States and Japan, The United States was adamant that Japan should withdraw from China while Japan would do no such thing, inevitably leading to conflict. On the 1st of December, Japan decided to attack the United States and the attack on Pearl Harbour followed on the 7th.

In 1945, after Japan's surrender, Tojo attempted suicide when threatened with arrest by the Allies, but despite this, he was tried on various counts of waging wars of aggression, in violation of international law, and of ordering inhumane treatment of prisoners of war and others. His loyalty to Emperor Hirohito was unwavering and therefore, at his trial, he claimed personal responsibility for the war in order to deflect attention from the Emperor. He was hanged as a war criminal on the 23rd of December 1948 along with six other wartime leaders.

Newly discovered American documents revealed that Tojo's remains after being cremated were flown out to sea where they were scattered to stop efforts to preserve them as objects of pilgrimage. Until these documents were uncovered, there were two theories about what had happened to Tojo's remains. Some believed that they had been stolen by rightwing activists to become a symbol of reverence while others believed that they were later blown up by left-wingers because they were a symbol of repression.

Tojo was not universally revered in Japan and there were protests when in 1978, his name, along with thirteen other war criminals, was commemorated at the shrine at Yasukuni which is dedicated to the memory of those who had fallen in service to the Imperial family.

Before the war in the Pacific got under way, the Allied commanders held the Japanese Army in contempt, but that view was quickly changed by the attack on Pearl Harbour, the sinking of the British battleships Repulse and Prince of Wales, and the taking of Hong Kong and Singapore. As the war progressed, the Allies quickly came to learn that: 'although some Japanese were captured, most fought until they were killed or committed suicide'. (Powers, D.) The mantra of *no surrender* also extended to Japan's civilian population. When Saipan in July

1944 was overrun by the Allies, they witnessed Japanese mothers clutching their children, hurling themselves off cliffs and it is thought that some 22,000 died that way. But why?

With the fall of Saipan imminent, Emperor Hirohito had issued an order that stated that all Japanese soldiers and civilians on Saipan were to commit suicide rather than surrender to the Americans. In addition, the Japanese Army had spread propaganda amongst the civilians that if they were captured or surrendered, they would be raped, tortured to death and even be the victims of cannibalism. Japanese soldiers were also told that if they became prisoners of war, they would suffer the death penalty.

This led to the Japanese Army making suicidal banzai charges and the civilians hurled themselves off cliffs, which came to be known as Suicide Cliff and Banzai Cliff. Mass suicides took place with whole families jumping to their deaths. Some who had children, would slice their throats before jumping, and others simply walked into the sea and drowned. Some families would cluster around a captured grenade with one of them designated to pull the pin.

In an effort to stop these upsetting suicides, the Americans used captured Japanese civilians, using loudspeakers, to assure their compatriots that they would be well treated if they surrendered and some did. The others through their commitment to Emperor Hirohito ignored what they were told and went ahead with their suicides.

Powers writes that during the 1920s, the Japanese military became 'uncontrollable' and the country was gripped 'by the politics of assassination'. The military saw war as a means of purifying the nation and ultimately, the world. Those complex times for Japan came from a mixture of its 'ancient warrior tradition, societal pressure, economic necessity and sheer desperation'. The Samurai code of ethics, known as Bushido, was behind the belief in no surrender. Japan's war with Russia, 1904–1905, saw returning Japanese prisoners treated as social outcasts and the Japanese military was determined not to let that happen again.

Powers describes the life of a Japanese soldier as 'brutal' through harsh beatings and being kicked senseless over trivial matters such as 'serving their superiors rice too slowly or using a vest as a towel'. (Powers).

That brutality and the contempt for those that surrendered was ingrained in the Japanese soldier and led to the Japanese atrocities, compounded by their belief in the racial inferiority of the Chinese and therefore, they had no qualms about how they were treated. And before those in the West express their anger and disgust at this, they need to remember how the slaves shipped to the West Indies and America were treated.

Donovan recounts that the Japanese soldiers stripped men who had been captured and tied them to trees for bayonet practice. Others who had been captured were tied to the front of roadblocks and when opposing forces advanced, the Japanese opened fire from behind the tethered men.

Many thousands of Chinese women were raped and then killed with their bodies defiled by bamboo stakes and bayonets. It is estimated that the number of Chinese citizens and prisoners of war who died was between 200,000 and 300,000, a figure disputed by the Japanese.

Those in the upper echelons of the Japanese Army wanted to reduce the open raping of Chinese women, not because they were concerned about them as such, but because they wanted to instill better discipline among their men and also to reduce the number who contracted sexually transmitted diseases.

There was also some concern that the family and friends of those raped would seek revenge either individually or be motivated to join guerilla forces. Japanese society had tolerated prostitution, of which geishas played a part, and so there was no opposition to the creation of brothels known as comfort stations. The Japanese could not recruit enough women to act as prostitutes in the comfort stations, so, inevitably Chinese women, and large numbers of Korean women, together with children were forced into prostitution, an occurrence that lasted until 1945, but also women from other countries the Japanese had invaded suffered the same fate. These women were 'raped thirty to forty times a day'. (Lewis and Steele)

In 2015, the Prime Minister of Japan officially apologised for the practice and agreed to pay a sum of 1 billion yen, or about $9 million, to the 46 surviving comfort women.

The incidence of rape did not decline as a result and nor did the numbers of soldiers contracting sexually transmitted diseases. Any prostitute working in a comfort station, who contracted a sexually transmitted disease, was forced to leave without any form of medical care. Once the war had ended, the Japanese offered to pay compensation to the women who had survived (and an estimate of the number who had died was 75% including those who committed suicide to escape) which appeared to be the right thing to do, but in reality, little was actually paid out.

The Japanese created Unit 731, also known as the Kwantung Army Epidemic, Prevention and Water Supply Unit, to carry out covert human experiments including biological and chemical warfare experiments. These experiments were carried out on Allied prisoners of war and those that survived were then executed. The Japanese researchers called those they were experimenting on as 'logs' because their bodies were burnt after death.

The prisoners were used in a variety of ways such as being infected with various diseases, and vivisection without anesthetics, to examine the effects of the disease. Any female prisoners would almost certainly have been raped before their experiments started. One experiment involved one prisoner being infected with syphilis and then forced to have sex with other prisoners. Others were made to suffer frostbite which was then left to turn gangrenous. Unit 731 gave typhoid-infected bread roles to Chinese prisoners of war and once it was clear that individuals were infected, they were released knowing that they would return to their family and friends and thereby spread the disease.

In other experiments, doctors would put people in pressure chambers to see how much pressure the human body could withstand before it exploded. All records that had been compiled during the war were destroyed shortly before and after the Japanese surrender, demonstrating clearly that they knew they had committed war crimes.

The main objective of these experiments was to develop chemical weapons with which the Japanese planned to bomb San Diego. Fortunately, the Japanese surrendered before that plan came to fruition.

Unit 1855 operated under the umbrella of Unit 731 and its objectives were to carryout experiments to ascertain the efficiency of the plague, typhus, cholera and other diseases if used as weapons against military and civilian personnel. The unit was based in Peking and employed both Korean and Chinese interpreters to translate when prisoners were brought in to be experimented on.

Prisoners were kept in designated wards depending on whether they were infected, not yet infected, or the disease was dormant. The interpreters were used by the Japanese doctors to ask questions about symptoms and to record the answers given. However, there was no attempt to alleviate the suffering which, eventually, would lead to the prisoner's death and indeed many of the interpreters became infected and died as well. These experiments stopped when the Japanese Army surrendered and once again, none of those involved were ever charged with war crimes.

Appendix 1 outlines a war crimes trial in Hong Kong (Case No:WO235/1012) which was one of 46 trials, involving 123 persons, who were tried in Hong Kong for war crimes committed during the Second World War. This particular trial involved the treatment of prisoners of war at the Sham Shui Po prisoner of war camp.

In the view of the Japanese Government, the conflict in China was no more than an incident rather than a war and therefore, the international conventions concerning Chinese prisoners of war did not apply and therefore, 'no problems will arise if we kill them or deport them'. This was the official line that enabled the Japanese army to commit its atrocities. The constraints of international law towards the treatment of Chinese prisoners were removed by a directive signed by Emperor Hirohito in August 1937.

Emperor Hirohito (1901–1989) was the 124th Emperor of Japan and reigned over the Empire of Japan from 1926 until 1947 after which he became Emperor of the State of Japan. Hirohito and his wife, Empress Kojun, had two sons and five daughters. During the Second World War, he was portrayed by the Japanese Government and military as a pacifist but in reality, he supported the Army's ambitions although his inherent caution made him nervous of the risks involved. He never spoke out against the Japanese Army's atrocities and indeed removed the constraints imposed by international law on the treatment of Chinese prisoners by signing a directive in August 1937.

By 1979, he was the only monarch in the world with the title 'Emperor' and one of the longest serving monarchs in the world. When he died, he was succeeded by his eldest son Akihito.

For example, General Kaiko-Sha, captured over 14,000 Chinese troops near the Chang Jiang River and he ordered his men to machine gun all of them, an event which took two full days to complete and which he recorded in his diary.

Japan did not believe in international conventions; so, for example, it refused to sign the Geneva Convention that banned the use of chemical weapons and therefore, its stance was that banning the use of such weapons did not apply to China. This is an interesting point because it shows that the Japanese Government was aware of the convention and had its excuse ready. The Japanese, therefore, were more than happy to use chemical weapons and Emperor Hirohito approved this by signing such orders in 1938 and agreed their use three hundred times.

The chemicals used included phosgene gas, chlorine gas, and mustard gas and for those familiar with the First World War, they will know that these were used on the Western Front which led to the banning of the use of chemical weapons under the Geneva Convention.

The Japanese Army did not keep records of those Chinese soldiers who surrendered and so it is not possible to say how many were in fact killed and after the surrender of Japan, a total of just fifty-six Chinese prisoners were released. After eight years of war that is a truly shocking figure however, the Japanese treated all prisoners of war cruelly, because having been captured or surrendered, they were viewed with the utmost contempt. The treatment of Allied prisoners is more widely known but that is not the case where Chinese prisoners are concerned.

Between February and March 1942, the Sook Ching Massacre took place following the capture of Singapore. It was a planned operation to kill Singapore's entire Chinese population and later this operation was extended to Malaysia. The Japanese later admitted that 5,000 Chinese had been killed – men, women and children – but it is thought that the true figure was nearer 70,000. The Japanese Army took those to be executed to designated killing sites and the methods used were varied – shot by firing squad, machine-gunned, beheaded or bayoneted.

From quite early on in the war, there were problems getting sufficient food supplies to the Japanese soldiers on the front line forcing them to turn to canni90allism. An order was issued by Major-General Aozu in November 1944 that stated that the consumption of enemy flesh was excluded from the list of military crimes. However, eating the flesh of a non-combatant was a military crime punishable by death. This aspect of Japanese behavior is covered in some detail in Lewis and Steele's book: *Hell in the Pacific*.

Here are two examples of how Allied prisoners were treated by the Japanese. On the 18th of April 1942, sixteen B-25 Mitchell Bombers too off from the USS Hornet, an aircraft carrier, for a retaliatory strike, known as the Doolittle Raid, on Tokyo, Kobe, Yokosuka, Nagoya, Kobe, and Osaka. It was a retaliatory strike following Japan's attack on Pearl Harbour. Concerned that the Japanese had spotted the US naval force, the planes had to take off 650 rather than 400 miles from the Japanese mainland and islands. While little real damage was caused by the raid, it helped to raise American morale while at the same time causing real concern for the Japanese because it showed that mainland Japan and its islands were then reachable.

After the raid, the bombers were meant to fly to China and land in areas controlled by the Chinese Nationalists but inevitably, they started to run out of fuel. While one plane diverted to the Soviet Union, the remaining fifteen either had to crash land or the crews bailed out. Eighty airmen were involved in the raid and while three were killed and eight captured by the Japanese, sixty managed to evade the Japanese with the help of local resistance groups.

The Japanese were desperate to capture these airmen and they scoured the coastal areas where the planes had landed. This resulted in the slaughter of thousands of men, women and children, Chinese civilians, on suspicion of helping the airmen. The eight captured airmen were put on trial and three were later executed by the firing squad.

The Special Operations Australia, also known as Force 137, mounted Operation Rimau in October 1944. Its objective was to sink Japanese shipping by attaching limpet mines in the Bay of Kepala. In subsequent gun battles with the Japanese Army, thirteen commandos were killed or died of their wounds in captivity. Eleven commandos were captured and put on trial on the 3rd of July 1945 on charges of perfidy and espionage. Inevitably, they were found guilty and sentenced to death and were executed by beheading on the 7th of July 1945, and their bodies were dumped in three unmarked graves.

Appendix 7 tells the story of a Thai gentleman named 'Boonpong' and how he smuggled items into Allied POW camps to help alleviate suffering there.

Towards the end of the war as Japanese prisoner of war camps were liberated, and stories of how the Japanese treated the prisoners of war started to come out. The British Government decided that the stories should not be made public; firstly because of the outrage that would follow and secondly, they might provoke the Japanese into committing more atrocities on the remaining prisoners of war as their defeat loomed larger as surrender became inevitable.

Despite clear evidence that Emperor Hirohito had been directly involved in many of the atrocities carried out, he was never charged with war crimes after the Japanese surrender. Emperor Hirohito was a god-like figure in Japan and therefore, charging him with war crimes and executing him would have led to a massive reaction from the Japanese people which the allies after years of war did not need. After all, is Iraq a safer or better place after the trial and execution of Saddam Hussein?

The Japanese atrocities in China would in all probability have been at the forefront of the minds of the Japanese delegation as they made their way through the courtyards of the Forbidden City for the signing of the surrender documents.

Even when Emperor Hirohito made his first ever broadcast to the Japanese people on the 14th of August 1945, bringing the war to an end, his speech never mentioned the words 'surrender' or 'defeat'.

It would be easy to argue that the history of wars is written by the victors and therefore, the books, films and the media do show these Japanese atrocities. However, Allied soldiers also committed atrocities both then and now but undoubtedly nowhere near the scale and volume of the Japanese soldiers.

The defeated countries in World War Two had their officer classes brought before courts in Nuremburg and Tokyo. Those alleged to have been committed by Allied soldiers occasionally led to courts martial but other incidents were either investigated and no further action was taken, or were simply swept under the carpet.

In the war in the Pacific, US soldiers also committed shocking and horrific things such as mutilating Japanese corpses including cutting off ears and in some cases, removing skulls, some of which were then sent home to family and friends (List verse.com). This led to the American Commander-in-Chief of the Pacific Fleet issuing directives against this in both 1942 and 1944.

The website of warhistoryonline.com states that American soldiers raped an estimated 10,000 women on the island of Okinawa, and some of these occurred after the Japanese surrender.

"No one in an SOE circuit was likely to be in a state to take and keep prisoners. Such barbarous habits as knee-capping left their victims unable to move and talk: not what SOE security demanded." (Foot, M.R.D.) The guerilla units who fought the Japanese could not afford to take prisoners, so they killed them as they lacked both food, medical supplies and prisoner of war camps.

Today, war crimes come before the International Criminal Court (ICC) in The Hague, Netherlands, and it recently issued a 180–page report which was covered on the BBC News website. The ICC report states: "It is without dispute there is evidence war crimes were committed." The report states that 'hundreds' of prisoners were abused by soldiers, some prisoners were raped or subjected to sexual violence. Others were beaten so badly they died from their injuries. When and where did this happen? This happened between the years 2003–2009 by British soldiers in Iraq.

Lewis and Steele wrote that the United Nations War Crimes Commission tried over 7,600 Japanese for a variety of crimes and executed around 900 mostly for atrocities against prisoners of war.

The book *Hell in the Pacific*, by Jonathan Lewis and Ben Steele, contains a number of eye-witness accounts of the atrocities committed by both the Japanese and the Allies.

Japan today is still very slippery in the ways that it deals with the issues of liability and compensation. In his book, *Nemesis*, Max Hastings writes about the attempt by Chinese labourers, some 30,000 were taken to Japan of whom some 7,000 died, who had been employed by 35 companies, a number of which are still trading. Some of these Chinese labourers brought a case against Mitsubushi and its defence team incredibly even questioned whether Japan had invaded China.

In the mid–1960s, an independent Singapore demanded that Japan should apologise and make reparations for the Sook Ching Massacre. The Japanese government agreed to pay 50 million dollars to Singapore – half in the form of a loan to be repaid – and yet refused to apologise for its actions.

In 1999, fifty-four years after the war had ended and frustrated by the Japanese Government's failure to pay compensation to British prisoners of war, the British Government made the payments itself.

In January 2021, the Times reported that the Seoul District Court in South Korea had ordered Japan to pay compensation to a group of former wartime sex slaves. The Japanese Government reacted angrily to the order to pay £67,000 to twelve comfort women. The twelve women were just a small group representing the 'hundreds of thousands who were forced into brothels for the Imperial Japanese Army'. The court made an order that made it possible to seize Japanese

Government assets to cover the compensation award. Unsurprisingly, Japan has refused to acknowledge the order claiming that the courts of one country cannot claim jurisdiction over the government of another and took no part in the court proceedings.

The court's judgement stated that:

"State immunity cannot be applied to crimes against humanity. Evidence, relevant materials and testimonies show that the victims suffered from extreme, unimaginable mental and physical pain due to the illegal acts of the accused." The article goes on to say: "Estimates of how many were abused run as high as 200,000. Thousands of women from China, Indonesia, Taiwan, the Philippines, Netherlands and South and North Korea claim to be former comfort women. They say they suffered rape, beatings and forced abortion. In South Korea, 16 survive with an average age above 90."

Japan had officially admitted the existence of the comfort brothels and also apologised. Some within the Japanese Government insist that the verbal testimony of elderly women is unconvincing. In 2015, the Japanese Prime Minister, Shinzo Abe, had apologised and paid 'more than £7 million into a fund for the benefit of surviving victims'. There was, however, one condition which was that South Korea must acknowledge that the issue was 'finally and irreversibly resolved'. Clearly, the South Korean Government have chosen to abandon that condition which will in turn exacerbate the tensions between the two countries.

The Japanese stance is that it is wrong for China with its own poor Human Rights record, to seek compensation from Japan.

On the 31st of March 2021, the Japanese Prime Minister became the first foreign leader to be welcomed into the White House by President Biden. These old enemies now share the same foreign policy agenda namely the threat from China. President Biden spoke about the challenges posed by China:

"We have to shore up American competitiveness to meet the stiff competition we're facing from an increasingly assertive China. We have to strengthen our alliances and work with like-minded partners to ensure that the rules of international norms that govern cyberthreats and emerging technologies that will shape our future are grounded in our democratic values, not those of autocrats."

The American view is that while it doesn't want to provoke China, it has to send a clear signal that some of the steps it is taking are undermining the peace and stability of the region.

9. Operation Ichigo

"An Atomic bomb has destroyed Hiroshima and Japan has capitulated."
(Newspaper headline 10 August 1945)

In December 1943, the Japanese embarked on an air offensive against American air bases which was then followed by a land campaign against Chinese forces based in East China.

In 1944, the Japanese launched Operation Ichigo, or 'Operation Number One', which involved a number of battles between the Japanese forces, attempting to sweep across central and South-East China, and the National Revolutionary Army of the Republic of China. Japan's primary objectives for the Campaign were to open a land route to French Indo-China and was seen as necessary to put a stop to America's B-29 bombers flying from airbases located on the Chinese coastal regions in the south and attacking the Japanese mainland and islands. If the campaign was successful, then Japanese troops would drive up the Yangtze Valley to seize the Chinese capital of Chungking, thereby forcing China out of the war.

As the Americans were forced to abandon their coastal airfields, the Office of Strategic Services (OSS) became heavily involved in denying the Japanese Army getting its hands on the supply dumps of the American airfields. At one abandoned airfield at Tusham, some 50,000 tons of material was destroyed.

The Operation lasted from April to December 1944. The three key battles were fought in the provinces of Henan, Hunan and Guangxi and were known as Operation Kogo, Operation Togo 1, Operation Togo 2 and Operation Togo 3.

The Republic of China authorities chose to ignore French intelligence that the Japanese were about to launch a fresh offensive, believing it to be Japanese 'fake news'. The Chinese believed that as only some 30,000 Japanese troops had crossed the Yellow River in Northern China, it was only a minor offensive, given that the front between the two armies had remained unchanged since the 1940s.

Chiang Kai-Shek believed that the crossing of the Yellow River was just a ploy, when in fact, it was the start of Operation Kogo, and that Japanese intentions lay elsewhere and therefore he withdrew some 400,000 soldiers in the face of the Japanese advance. To his surprise, the number of Japanese soldiers quickly grew to nearer 500,000 across a front of 120 miles. In addition to the 500,000 men, the Japanese had 15,000 vehicles, 6,000 artillery pieces, 800 tanks and 100,000 horses. Chinese troops that had been used at Tushan to fight the Chinese Communists had to be redeployed to fight the Japanese. The Japanese crossed the Yellow River into Hunan Province. To make matters worse, Chiang Kai-Shek's best troops were in Burma.

Chiang Kai-Shek quickly withdrew 34 Nationalist divisions and therefore the Chinese defensive line was quickly overrun and it is estimated that for every Japanese soldier killed, the Chinese Army suffered forty losses. The Allied forces quickly came to realise that Chiang Kai-Shek regularly overstated his problems in an effort to gain more aid from them – and they largely ignored him.

Operation Kogo involved 390,000 Chinese troops, led by General Tang Enbo, to defend the strategic position of Luoyang. In late April, the Japanese crossed the Yellow River and defeated the Chinese at Xuchang and then started to besiege Luoyang on 13 May and finally took it on 25 May.

> **General Tang Enbo (1898–1954) was a Chinese Nationalist general who was one of the Kuomintang generals most feared and respected by the Japanese during the war in China. He was a graduate of the Imperial Japanese Army Academy, and therefore, was familiar with the tactics of the Japanese Army during the war with China. However, due to the decisions made by Chiang Kai-Shek, he was not as effective as a general as he might have been.**

May saw the second phase of the Japanese campaign get underway. The Japanese advance was just as destructive for the Chinese civilians as it was for the Chinese Army as it caused thousands of deaths of Chinese civilians in the regions of Hunan, Quangdong, Guangxi and Guizhou largely due to exacerbating the famine they were already suffering. This led to the Chinese Army unexpectedly experiencing attacks from its own people, notably Henan civilians. The Henan civilians attacked the Chinese Army and disarmed some 50,000 Chinese soldiers and stole guns, bullets, explosives, mortars and radio equipment. In the majority of cases, the Chinese soldiers offered little resistance as they had had enough of the fighting. Chiang Kai-Shek issued orders that any commanders who retreated should be shot, however, his order made little difference.

As the Chinese Army advanced, the civilians retreated from the villages taking with them any stored grain and leaving the villages and the fields empty which meant that the Army had to go without food for several days. One Chinese General stated that the damage done by the Hunan civilians was greater than that inflicted by the Japanese Army which, in turn, was being attacked by the civilians with weapons taken from the Chinese Army. The Japanese advance started to slow not because of that resistance but due to logistical problems of keeping its frontline supplied.

In late 1944, two Chinese divisions to the north of the country were noticeably performing better than their comrades elsewhere, thanks to General Stilwell who wanted them to re-open a land route into China. Stilwell had overseen these troops being flown to India for training where they were kept well away from Nationalist corruption and incompetence. The men responded well as they were fed, unlike elsewhere in the Nationalist Army where officers would routinely take their food from them, they were paid by the United States and enjoyed the benefits of air support.

Kweillin was taken by the Japanese on the 10th of November 1944. In the build up to the city being taken, all of its citizens, who wanted to leave and could do so, left in thousands on train, boats and on foot. The city was also home to the United States Airforce's largest airfield at Liangtang. In the time available before the Japanese overran the city, all the airfield's buildings were destroyed, every gallon of fuel, and every piece of equipment, that could be was removed. The equipment that remained was blown up and burned to stop it from falling into Japanese hands.

The Chinese Nationalist Army confidently assured the Americans that it could defend the city but as previously commented on, it was not properly armed or disciplined to prepare the city's defences. Therefore, the Japanese 11th Army quickly took the city and moved on towards Chungking thereby joining up with troops from the east and Indo-China, thereby cutting China in two.

By December, the Japanese had reached Indo-China, which was an important objective of the operation, and their advance came to a halt. As a result, the US Airforce bases moved inland from the coast and continued to bomb the Hunan – Guangxi railway between Hengyang and Luizhou that the Japanese had established after the first phase of the campaign.

The Japanese campaign failed to achieve its long term aims. It did, however, bring about the enforced move of the American airbases from the Chinese coastal region to inland China, and this disrupted the Strategic B-29 bombers attacking the Japanese home islands but only for a short time. The effect of this Japanese success was neutralised when the Americans captured Saipan and the attacks on the Japanese homeland recommenced including firebombing Tokyo during 1944–45.

Due to the number of casualties, estimated at some 23,000, and issues with food supplies, Japan was forced to end Operation Ichigo. Chiang Kai-Shek then began to withdraw Chinese troops from the Burma theatre in order to launch his own offensive named: *White Tower* or *Iceman*, against the Japanese in East China. However, the Nationalist Army was also weakened, having suffered some 500,000 to 600,000 casualties (Hsiung, J.) General Wedemeyer then ordered the remaining Chinese troops in Burma be returned to defend the city of Chihkiang which in turn was important in the defence of Chungking. However, the Japanese campaign was not renewed although in April 1945, the Japanese did attack Chihkiang but were defeated by a combination of the American airforce and the American trained and equipped Chinese army.

With the Nationalist forces weakened, General Stilwell was determined to oust Chiang Kai-Shek, given that the two of them had never really got on, and take control of the Nationalist armed forces. To do this, he had to persuade General George Marshall to convince President Roosevelt to send Chiang Kai-Shek an ultimatum threatening that if he refused to place General Stilwell in command of the Nationalist forces then he would end all American aid.

When Roosevelt's ultimatum arrived, Stilwell delivered it immediately to Chiang Kai-Shek. This was despite pleas from Patrick Hurley, the President's Special Envoy to China, to delay the ultimatum and through diplomacy achieve what Stilwell wanted but in a manner that would be more acceptable to Chiang Kai-Shek.

Chiang Kai-Shek saw the ultimatum as a threat to China's independence and in a formal reply, insisted that Stilwell should be replaced immediately and replaced by another US general. As a result, Stilwell was replaced by Major General Wedemeyer, as both Chiang Kai-Shek's Chief of Staff and Commander of the US forces in China. Although Chaing Kai-Shek had got his way, it caused damage to his regime. The New York Times war correspondent, Brooks Atkinson, wrote:

"The decision to relieve General Stilwell represents the political triumph of a moribund, anti-democratic regime that is more concerned with maintaining its political supremacy than in driving the Japanese out of China. The Chinese Communists... have good armies that they are claiming to be fighting guerrilla warfare against the Japanese in North China – actually they are covertly or even overtly building themselves up to fight Generalissimo's government forces... The Generalissimo naturally regards these armies as the chief threat to the country and his supremacy... has seen no need to make sincere attempt to arrange at least a truce with them for the duration of the war... No diplomatic genius could have overcome the Generalissimo's basic unwillingness to risk his armies in battle with the Japanese."

As a result, the United States lost confidence in their Chinese allies, and therefore, the China-Burma-India theatre lost its priority and the United States turned towards defeating the Japanese by taking island after island that stood between its forces and Japan's mainland.

The Chinese Communists had played no part in the campaign because its leadership was planning for the inevitable civil war once the Japanese were defeated, and with the Nationalists weakened by the Ichigo Campaign, there was every chance that they would be in a better position to win power.

The SOE planned with the North Chinese War Zone Commander, Marshall Hu Zongnan, to form a guerilla army to work behind the Japanese lines. It was agreed that the SOE would provide 'officers, signal officers, communications, weapons and equipment'. In fact, Major Stanfield was the only signal officer posted to the guerilla army and he travelled about 1,000 miles north to Sian with Chinese General Ho.

Sian is where the Terracotta Army was found in 1974.

The objective was to prepare the guerilla army as much as possible. Captain Stanfield established wireless stations in Sian and along the Yellow River, opposite the Japanese lines, with small wireless sets with Chinese operators who had been trained by the SOE.

Marshall Hu Zongnan (1896–1962) was a general in both the National Revolutionary and the Republic of China Armies and was one of Chiang Kai-Shek's most trusted generals. He retreated to Taiwan with Chiang Kai-Shek in 1949, who became President, where he acted as his Military Strategy Adviser until his death in 1962.

Later, when Captain Stanfield had returned to Sian, he attended a dinner attended by the Provincial Governor Hu, Chinese generals and officials. The dinner was disturbed by crowds gathering outside to the extent that General Ho sent a boy out to find out what was going on. He returned with a newspaper dated 10th of August that carried the headline *An Atomic bomb has destroyed Hiroshima and Japan has capitulated.*

For most of August with the war effectively ended, Stanfield spent as much time as he could buying up works of art and Chinese artefacts including a Nestorian Tablet which is the oldest Christian tablet in China, commemorating the coming of the Nestorian Christians to Sian in 635 AD.

In a letter dated the 31st of August, Stanfield wrote: "From the world's least known corner of the war, this place has suddenly had a few gleams thrown at it. All the North China prisoners of war camps are being supplied by US air from here. Last night we heard on the BBC news of Corporal Heather being the first British POW by air from Hong Kong being freed. Actually, he came here from North China and stayed in this compound. We had a good chat. He was amazingly fit considering all his experiences."

This stopped all further plans for dealing with the Japanese and Major Stanfield and the others waited for the hoped-for orders to travel to Peking which is where the Japanese Civil Government of China was located. Sian was 600 miles from Peking, and no road or rail travel was available and so the US Airforce flew them instead. At the time, the Japanese Civil Government was based in Peking.

Orders had arrived for Colonel Bridge and Captain Stanfield to fly to Peking with Chinese General Ho. At that time, there was no road or rail travel available for the six-hundred-mile journey from their base at Sian to Peking. As a result, they flew, courtesy of the American Airforce:

"After packing up, we went to the airfield where the US Airforce was in control and were directed to take the next available plane for Peking. The first we looked into was jammed with freight and the pilot very sensibly refused to take onboard anymore. The next one was comparatively clear and we boarded."

They arrived in Peking on the 14th of September. When they landed, they were greeted by Japanese officers 'still strutting around with their swords'. They were met by what Stanfield described as 'superb limousines' which took them to the Grand Hotel De Peking, which was to be their base. That evening, there was a Victory Dance Night at the hotel attended by more than a thousand people.

In a letter dated the 19th of September, Stanfield wrote about the British Legation:

"The British Legation is an absolute pearl. There is a little church, which takes you back to an English village. To take back the British Embassy, we had a flag-raising ceremony with the visiting British General, Colonel Bridge and myself with a few British residents."

The re-opening of the British Embassy was an important part of preparing for the arrival of the Ambassador, Sir Horace Seymour, and his staff.

> **Sir Horace James Seymour, GCMG CVO (1885–1978) was a diplomat who served as the British Ambassador to China, based in Chungking from 1942–46. He retired in 1947.**

In the days leading up to the surrender ceremony, Stanfield found himself invited to 'lunch, dinner and tea and numerous parties' because at that time, he was the most senior British officer in Peking because by the 4th of October, Colonel Bridge had gone to see his family in Shanghai where they had been interned.

Captain Stanfield had continued his interest in Chinese artifacts as he wrote in a letter dated the 4th of October:

"I was in at the kill when one of the internees Maurice Gordon, managed to get one of the treasures of China. I cannot say anything to the Chinese about it, as Prince Ni's family, who disposed of the painting would lose an awful lot of face.

The family needed money quickly and Gordon had an artist go-between. The painting is Emperor Chien Lung in the Hunting Park and has his own writing in the beginning. It is a famous painting and was given to the Prince by Pu Yi (the last Emperor). The price asked was the sum they required: $380,000, worth about £40, but as the painting is historical it is really priceless. It is all on Imperial Silk.

It is in a huge roll and is 17 feet long, plus 35 feet extra calligraphy etc. The beginning is worked in gold thread with dragons. Quite unique. I would put it on a par with the Bayeaux Tapestry. It would be impossible to buy, Americans would pay anything for it. Gordon will probably lend it to the British Museum."

In the end, Stanfield did not buy this piece of history, feeling that after all Maurice had gone through in the camps, he 'deserves to get something good'.

Before leaving Sian, Stanfield attended the Official Victory Celebration. "We were bidden to a dance and supper, given by the local authorities, the War Zone Commander Marshall Hu Zung Nan and the Provincial Governor. They did things well. There was tremendous excitement and enthusiasm in the streets and crackers and rockets went off all night. Still, one cannot compose oneself for peace very easily and the problems China has to face make her serious people heavy hearted."

Stanfield wrote to his family on the 11th of December 1945 and told them that he was leaving Peking the following day and that he may have to revert to the rank of Captain. The decision about his rank would be known when he arrived in Chungking and there, he found out that he would retain his rank until demobilisation.

In the few days before his departure, General Sir Adrian Carton de Wiart and Lady Seymour, the Ambassador's wife, had arrived in Peking for a short stay. Stanfield was invited to what he described as a very stately lunch at the French Embassy for the General and Lady Seymour:

"There were 18 of us seated around the table, rows of glasses, the crested Embassy plate was out for the occasion. The meal was most imposing. So of course, is the General – the most wounded British General. One eye, one hand, and one foot and a VC. He is the Prime Minister's representative to China."

Lieutenant General Sir Adrian Carton de Wiart VC, KBE, CB, CMG, and DSO (1880–1963) was the most wounded and decorated British General having lost his left eye, left hand and one foot. He had served in the Boer War, and the First and Second World Wars.

After a long and distinguished military career, he was appointed from October 1943 until retirement in 1946, the British

---

> **Government's Military Representative with General Chiang Kai-Shek in China.**

Stanfield left Peking by plane on the 12th of December 1945 and was 'seen off by the Mayor of Peking and other dignitaries'. The plane had a short stop in Shanghai and arrived in Chungking on the 13th only to find they couldn't land due to fog and so were diverted to Kunming. The party was met by men from Force 136 and was then taken to its office and compound.

After a meal Stanfield: "drove a jeep to our station on the other side of the lake to see Philip Smith, whom I had not seen for six months He was in the process of closing down and I learnt that at the end of the month, I would be posted to Hong Kong Signals. I suppose a better job than hanging around in India for repatriation. Philip is going home as he has been out here nearly five years. I am sorry to be parting but he will be around in England."

Stanfield and the others left Kunming early in the morning of the 14th and arrived in Chungking 'about mid-day'. By the 20th, Stanfield was in Hong Kong and took up his post of 'Royal Signals, OC, Hong Kong Signal Company'. He did not find his new company particularly easy writing:

"My company is in the Hong Kong Jockey Club in Happy Valley. The house is good but bare. The troops are mainly Indian with four British Section Officers. The first job I have is to Chair a Court Martial, in which I am the sole Judge, with power to give up to one year in prison. Rather a responsibility. It is only in the Indian Army that one is able to do this. (I doubt I will give the full sentence even if I find him guilty, perhaps a reprimand.)"

He described his role as follows:

"There were four sections of Indians with British officers. The work was mostly administrative and as there were different Indian races involved, was quite complicated. I was doing a holding job, until the official company HQ arrived from India. This happened after a few months; much to my relief, I was then given a Staff job in Land Force HQ."

On the 26th, Stanfield was invited to lunch at Lady Seymour's residence. "The spread was very good – everything rationed was in profusion." That evening he went to a party "at the GOC's. We got there too early and found ourselves surrounded by Colonels and Generals. They were soon diluted and we found ourselves jammed in a crowd of all the British Chungking residents.

Again, the buffet supper was magnificent. Where all the turkeys, hams, ice cream and all the other food came from is a mystery."

In a letter dated the 6th of January 1946, he wrote: "Force 136 is closing down in China. I hope to be back in England by June and then finish with the Army for good." By the middle of January, he was writing that the SOE in China had closed down.

The HQ for the Signal Company had now arrived from India and Stanfield was offered a post on the staff as Captain for the remaining two months before he travelled back to England, although he retained his post as Major until his demobilisation as that had already been agreed.

As a result of the HQ being relocated to Hong Kong, Stanfield would no longer be OC of the Hong Kong Signal Company and his position was to be taken over by "a regular, an ex-Sergeant Major who was now a Major. He is a good chap, if one is able to ignore his language. I am glad he is not my CO. I am relieved in a way, as the Company is made up mostly of Indians and they are complicated to administer. Sikhs, Madrassis, Dogras etc., all with different foods, customs, and languages."

By the 9th of April, Stanfield had taken up the post of Chief Signal Officer at the HQ. This involved him moving from the Jockey Club to the CSO's mess, which was near the Land Force HQ, halfway up the peak, however, he would be sailing back to England three weeks later.

On the 16th of May, Stanfield embarked on the SS Salween to begin his journey home and by the 24th, he was in Singapore waiting for his ship home. He finally returned on the SS Strathmore, 'a crowded troop ship', via Suez and the Mediterranean to Southampton.

"After disembarkation leave, we waited for demobilisation. This happened for me at Thirsk, where each was given a complete set of civilian clothes and a gratuity. This was calculated on the time spent in each rank held – as Signalman, Officer Cadet, 2nd Lieutenant, Lieutenant, Captain, Major. This added up to £118. But the pay continued for the three months' demobilisation leave at Major's rates."

John Stanfield and his sister, Audrey had planned to enter Cambridge University together in September 1946 "she at Girton College and I at Trinity College. Audrey to read Natural Sciences and I Economics, and then Theology, after being accepted by the Methodist Ministry." However, in an addendum to his book *War Letters Home*, 1941–1946, he wrote:

"I had a hiccup getting out of the army. I had my place in Trinity College, expecting to get out in time for the September term." A GHQ order suddenly said, "Too many Signals officers are going at once. Signal officer's demobilisation will be delayed three months." Fortunately, my father's MP happened to be the Minister of War. The reply to a letter from me was "Major Stanfield Royal Signals will be demobilised forthwith."

"The war was over. So back to school after six years and having signed the final official ending of World War Two in China." After four years at Trinity College, Cambridge, John Stanfield was ordained in the Methodist Ministry and then went to Gambia in West Africa for seven years.

10. Aftermath – Part 1

"The period that follows an unpleasant event or accident, and the effects that it causes."
(Cambridge English Dictionary.)

The Chinese Nationalists and the Chinese Communists can be defined by the two men who led them – Chiang Kai-Shek and Mao Tse-Tung. Both men were similar in a number of ways. Both were ruthless, focused on gaining power, whatever the expense to the people and the country, and were more interested in fighting each other, rather than defeating the Japanese.

*****

The civil war between the Communists and the Nationalists had been reignited following the defeat of Japan. There was friction also between members of the Communist leadership.

In August 1945, Soviet troops had crossed the Amur River into Manchuria and thanks to the railway, they could progress some fifty miles a day. Mao was looking to a general Communist uprising across the whole of China, not just in the countryside but also in the cities. Mao's Red Army now had 900,000 troops spread out across Northern China and he then planned his first move which was to send 3,000 undercover soldiers into the cities to stir up rebellion. However, Stalin intervened and told Mao to pull back for the simple reason that he was worried about America's atomic capability and a variety of independent revolutionary movements that had sprung up in China and Japan.

Strategically, Stalin decided to declare his support for Chiang Kai-Shek and sent Mao a letter telling him to put a halt to open clashes with the Nationalists. The signing of a Sino-Soviet treaty in August 1945 reassured Chiang Kai-Shek and he therefore invited Mao to take part in the peace negotiations. The Americans wanted Chiang Kai-Shek to talk to Mao about peace. Mao did not trust Chiang Kai-Shek and feared for his safety and twice turned down an invitation to go to Chongqing. Mao then said that he would send Chou En-lai in his place but Chiang Kai Shek insisted that Mao had to be present while at the same time, Stalin had also told Mao that he should go. Stalin was secretly helping Mao to seize territory but he was worried that if Mao did not go and take part in the peace negotiations then the Americans would see it as him rejecting peace and would then support Chaing Kai-Shek.

With very little choice, Mao went by plane on the 28th of August, accompanied by the American Ambassador, Patrick Hurley, to Chongquing where he was to stay for six weeks. Hurley also suggested that if Chiang Kai-Shek and Mao agreed a peace deal then he would bring them both to the White House. While in Chongquing, Mao behaved with great diplomacy and said that he supported Chiang Kai-Shek, but it was all an act. He wanted to rule China but he knew that would only be achieved via a civil war. Chiang Kai-Shek was also playing a part in that he, too, wanted to rule China and knew that the route to that was a civil war but he needed the Americans to think that he supported peace. With the Americans satisfied, at least in the short term, US forces occupied the northern cities of Peking and Tianjin and helped to move the Nationalist troops to Manchuria.

On the 10th of October when the Japanese Surrender Ceremony was taking place in Peking, and was also the anniversary of the 1911 Revolution, Mao made a speech committing to peace while knowing that clashes were taking place across the countryside, and on the flight back telling his comrades that the agreement was nothing more than a scrap of paper.

The Soviet forces left China in June 1946, leaving the Communists and the Nationalists to restart their civil war which saw 'hundreds of thousands of troops clash with air and artillery support, sometimes in temperatures of -20 C'. (Farrell)

After 1947, the war was fought on two main fronts – Northern China and in central China in the provinces of Shandong, Anhui and Hunan. During this time, Mao was able to recruit a million men into the Red Army and was gaining support through his land reforms. While Mao's fortunes were on the up, Chiang Kai-Shek was struggling, despite a $400 million handout under the July 1948 China Aid Act.

The Nationalists were struggling due to 'corruption and incompetence, ordinary troops being poorly paid and provisioned while Nationalist supply lines were over-extended'. (Farrell). The sale of bonds and taxation only covered a small part of the War's expenses leaving the Government little choice but to print money resulting in rampant inflation. 'By 1947, nominal prices were 30,000 times above those of 1936. Much weaponry and other military supplies ended up on the black market'. (Farrell)

The Communists were the party of the countryside, whereas the Nationalists were more urban where they held control of the cities. With the Communists now in the ascendancy, their strategy was to mount sieges on the cities. The city of Shenyang with a population in normal times of some 1,200,000 saw that number swell to four million following the influx of refugees. Chennault, the US Airforce General, sent planes to evacuate people but could only rescue some 1,500 a day, leaving the rest to starve and suffer disease.

In May 1948, the Communists mounted a siege of Changchun which was to last 150 days. Again, many tens of thousands of civilians died from starvation and disease, with many dying through being caught in the crossfire between the Communists and the city walls.

The Nationalists were forced into retreat, and General Fu Zuoyi, commander of their troops in Northern China, took his troops into Peking, The Communists again surrounded the city and cut off both water and electricity supplies. Behind the days of being under siege, General Zuoyi had begun secret negotiations with Lin Biao the Communist commander which led, after forty days, to the signing of a surrender document on the 22nd of January 1949.

Lin Biao (1907–1971) was a Marshal of the People's Republic of China who played a key role in the Communist victory during the Chinese Rebellion of 1931 to 1945, especially in North-East China. Lin was the general who commanded the decisive Liaoshen and Pingjin Campaigns, in which he co-led the Manchurian Field Army to victory and led the People's Liberation Army into Peking. He crossed the Yangtze River in 1949, decisively defeated the Nationalists and took control of the coastal provinces in South-East China. He ranked third among the Ten Marshals. In 1971, he allegedly plotted to assassinate Mao Zedong and seize power. He died in September 1971 with Chinese government announcing that Lin was killed in an airplane crash in Mongolia as he was fleeing to the Soviet Union.

General Fu Zuoyi (1895–1974) was a Nationalist General who was the Commander-in-Chief stationed in Peking to guard the ancient city against a Communist takeover. Little did he realise that his defeat

---

and the surrender of the city would come about by the betrayal of his own daughter.

In 1946, the peace negotiations between the Communists and the Nationalists broke down. Unbeknown to General Fu, Communist agents were embedded within his inner circle including his daughter, Fu Dongju. The Communists ordered Fu Dongju to steal all her father's confidential documents and she bribed her five-year-old brother with chocolate to get General Fu's safe key thereby allowing her to photograph its contents and pass them to the Communists.

Fu Dongju took every opportunity to discourage her father from fighting against the Communist Party and sold further information to the CCP. As a result, Fu Zuoyi finally had to accept the secret peace talks proposed by the CCP and surrender his garrison of a quarter million men. He could not fight for his city, and he opened the gates to the Communist Army, allowing it to Peking on 31 January 1949.

General Fu came to understand the role his daughter had played, thereby causing a complete breakdown in their relationship. General Fu Zuoyi died of ill health in April 1974.

The Communists then focused on the Nationalist capital of Nanjing having mobilised, through conscription quotas imposed on every village, over one million men.

*****

By the 10th of January 1949, with the civil war at an end, Mao's Red Army, known as the 'People's Liberation Army', had entered Peking and Mao had proclaimed victory for the People's Republic of China (PRC) triumphantly in the city's Tiananmen Square. Mao's band of peasants and fugitives from 1927 had, by 1949, become rulers of China, the most populated country in the world. For Mao, victory had been a combination of politics and strategy. The Chinese Communist Party had its roots in the countryside supported by the peasantry, which constituted the largest part of the Chinese community, and to retain its support, the Communists embarked on a programme of land reform. The

Communists took a different approach to the peasantry treating it with less brutality and less corruption than was the case with the Nationalists. Overall, the Communists were no longer second best.

As a result, in 1949, Chiang Kai-Shek and the Nationalists (Republic of China) were forced by the Chinese Communists to retreat south. For some weeks, Chiang Kai-Shek and his other Nationalist leaders held out at Guangzhou, a port in the south of China, but on the 10th of December 1949, he flew to Taiwan, an island about one hundred miles from the Chinese mainland. The Republic of China (ROC) also governs twenty-two islands in the Taiwan Group and sixty-four islands to the west in the Pescadores archipelago. A further two islands, Matsu and Qemoy are situated just off the coast of China's mainland province of Fujian.

The Communists proved unstoppable elsewhere as well. In October 1949, the Communists gained control of the oil-rich province of Xinjiang which was also rich in coal, gold, and uranium. Tibet fell to the Communists in October 1950 when the People's Liberation Army entered the country and defeated its small army. The Tibetans had been caught off guard as at the time, they were negotiating with the People's Republic of China.

11. Aftermath – Part 2

"Re-unification of the nation must be realised and it will definitely be realised"
(President Xi Jinping)
*"But there should be absolutely no illusions that the Taiwanese people will
bow to pressure. We will continue to bolster our national defence and
demonstrate our determination to defend ourselves in order to ensure that
nobody can force Taiwan to take the path that China has laid out for us."*
(President Tsai Ing-wen, Taiwan.)

Chiang Kai-Shek ruled Taiwan as a strict one-party state. The Nationalists'
objective still remains to bring about the unification of mainland China and
Taiwan. Unfortunately for the Nationalists, the Chinese Communists and The
Peoples' Republic of China, had the same objective. The Chinese Government's
view is that Taiwan ceased to exist after the civil war and the founding of the
People's Republic of China.

The Taiwanese people have increasingly identified themselves as Taiwanese
rather than Chinese and their President, Tsai Ing-wen, is seen as someone who
wants to declare formal independence which, in turn, ratchets up the sabre
rattling.

While the People's Republic of China (PRC) claims Taiwan, there are also
territorial disputes with other countries. The Diayutai group of islands is also
claimed by both Japan and the PRC while the Paracels islands are claimed by
both the PRC and Vietnam. In addition, the Spratley Islands are claimed by the
PRC, Vietnam, Malaysia and the Philippines.

The Nationalists had been formed by Sun Yatsen who had, ironically,
organised it based on the Soviet Union. Both the Nationalist Government under
Chiang Kai-Shek and the Communist Government under Mao Tse-tung, shared
similarities with previous dynasties in that they both had their concentration of
power with a central point of authority.

*****

China became the world's largest economy in 2014 just sixty-five years after the Communists defeated the Nationalists. How had the Chinese Government been able to change the country from one of emperors, warlords, and peasants to the largest economy in the world? In the late 1960s, with his influence weakening, Mao sought to reassert his leadership with The Great Proletarian Cultures Revolution which led to purges and he unleashed the Red Guards which nearly led to another civil war.

> **The Great Proletarian Cultures Revolution (1966–1976) took place under the mantra *Fight selfishness, criticise revisionism*. The Cultural Revolution, formally the Great Proletarian Cultural Revolution, was launched by Mao Zedong and was a violent sociopolitical purge movement. Its stated objective was to preserve Chinese Communism by purging remnants of capitalist and traditional elements from Chinese society, and to re-impose Mao Zedong's thoughts as the dominant ideology. The Revolution marked Mao's return to the central position of power in China after a period in which Mao made a deliberate effort to eliminate those in the leadership who, over the years, had dared to cross him. The victims, from throughout the party hierarchy, suffered more than mere political disgrace. All were publicly humiliated and detained for varying periods, sometimes, under very harsh conditions; many were beaten and tortured, and not a few were killed or driven to suicide.**

Mao died in 1976 and the system of governance and Maoism died with him. Mao had introduced the rapid industrialisation of China which had caused the largest man-made famine in history, as it took peasants off the land and into factories and was also responsible for forty million deaths between the years 1959–1962.

Mao was succeeded by Den Xiaoping who set about dismantling the centralised command economy he had inherited. Today, China is a powerhouse of capitalism flooding markets with cheap consumer goods.

Den Xiaoping (1904–1997) became the most powerful figure in the People's Republic of China from the late 1970s until his death in 1997. During the Sino-Japanese war, he was an army commander and in the civil war that followed, he clinched the Communist victory by winning the Huai-Hai campaign. In the early 1950s, Mao brought him to Peking as part of the party's core leadership.

At this stage, he was loyal to Mao until the Mao-created famine when he started to distance himself from the leadership. Mao tried many times to keep Deng within the party leadership but failed leading to Deng's house arrest in 1967 and his later exile from Peking. Following the damage done to his family during this period – his eldest son threw himself from a window and ended up paralysed from the chest down – Deng turned his back on both Stalinism and Maoism. In 1973, Mao had Deng brought to Peking and installed him as a vice-premier and later put him in charge of the army which saw Deng once again becoming a member of the Polit bureau. During this period, Deng kept his revisionist ideas to himself and when Mao died in 1976, he became the country's leader. He then started to abandon many orthodox Communist doctrines and sought to introduce elements of capitalism such as a free enterprise system. Deng was also the architect of China's one-child policy, introduced to slow down the growth of the population.

Under his leadership, China, the country acquired a rapidly growing economy, rising standards of living, considerably expanded personal and cultural freedoms, and growing ties to the world economy.

*****

And, what of Peking, renamed as Beijing after 1979? Hedda Morrison, who took the photographs of the Peking surrender ceremony, had lived in Peking since 1933 when she took on the management of Hartungs Photo Studio. Morrison had completed her studies at the State Institute for Photography in Munich and wanted to work overseas when she saw an advertisement for a job at Hartungs. Peking appealed to her, so despite the modest salary and long hours, 'seven o'clock in the morning to six o'clock in the evening, six days a week, with unpaid overtime whenever special work had to be completed quickly'.

Hedda Morrison (1908–1991) was born Hedda Hammer in Stuttgart, Germany and she attended the State Institute for Photography in Munich. She then assisted photographers Adolf Lazi and Olga Linekelman before moving to Peking in 1933.

From then until the 1960s, she became famous for her photographs of Peking (Beijing), Hong Kong and Sarawak during the years 1930–1960. In 1940, she met Alistair Morrison, a correspondent for The Times and they married in Peking in 1946. In 1967, they moved to Canberra, where the couple lived until she died in 1991.

The Hedda Morrison Photographs of China 1933–1946, a collection of 5000 photographs and 10000 negatives, are held at the Harvard-Yenching Library. Major publications by Morrison include Travels of a photographer in Peking (1987), A photographer in Old Peking (1985), Life in a Longhouse (1962), and Sarawak (1957).

Morrison remained at Hartungs until her contract ran out in 1938 and then worked for an English lady, Miss Beiber, which enabled her to see a great deal of Peking and provided opportunities for her to take her photographs. She left Peking in 1946 but returned in 1948 and then again in 1979 and 1982 when she wrote:

"The changes that had taken place were enormous. The Peking that I knew is now no more than the core of a huge metropolis spreading out in every direction to cover what used to be agricultural land. There has been large scale industrialisation and nowadays, when you look out from cherished viewpoints of times past, you see a panorama of in multi-storey buildings punctuated by tall factory buildings belching smoke. The splendid city walls have been razed and the moat filled in to provide room for a ring road. The brilliant North China light has lost its shine to a layer of smog."

*****

Chiang Kai-Shek experienced further humiliation in 1971 when the United Nations agreed to restore all the rights to the Peoples' Republic of China as 'the only legitimate representatives of China to the UN'. The United Nations

Declaration (Appendix 6) went on to say that it would 'expel forthwith the representatives of Chiang Kai-Shek from the places which they unlawfully occupy at the United Nations and in all the organisations related to it'.

*****

China believes Taiwan's democratically elected government is bent on declaring independence, which is very much a red line for Beijing, as it sees Taiwan as a breakaway province that **will** eventually be part of China again. Meanwhile, Taiwan's President Tsai Ing-wen says Taiwan is already an independent country, provocatively called the Republic of China, which is Taiwan's formal name. Beijing considers Taiwan to be an integral part of its territory and argues strongly against any suggestions to the contrary.

On the 28th of April 2021, the Sky News website carried a report under the heading *We will defend ourselves to the very end*. The report said that Taiwan Foreign Minister, Joseph Wu had made this vow as 'China Prepares Final Assault':

"This is our country, this is our people and this is our way of life. We will defend ourselves to the very end."

Taiwan has never declared itself to be an independent state, although it has its own government, military and elections, and Joseph Wu reiterated that formal independence was not his government's intention – merely the preservation of the currently ambiguous status quo while China has vowed to claim it by force, if necessary and particularly if the territory makes a formal withdrawal from China itself.

In Taiwan, there is a generational split over what to do. Its younger generation supports the ruling Democratic Progressive Party (DPP), which generally supports Taiwan independence and which won the last election by a landslide. The older generation tends to support the Nationalist Party (KMT) which advocates a peaceful unification with China and is less in favour of provoking Beijing.

The United States Secretary of State, Antony Blinken, issued a statement early in May 2021, in which he said: "Taiwan is a reliable partner, a vibrant democracy, and a force for good in the world." China's reaction was threatening:

"Taiwan independence is a dead end. We have the determination and ability to thwart all Taiwan independence separatist activities, resolutely defend national sovereignty and territorial integrity, and resolutely safeguard the common interests of compatriots on both sides of the strait."

China has made it clear that it will not engage in diplomacy with any country that establishes formal ties with Taiwan and this has resulted in only fourteen countries plus the Vatican having a relationship with it. Its formal diplomatic links are with Swaziland, Vatican City, Haiti, Saint Kitts and Nevis, Saint Lucia, Saint Vincent and Grenadines, Belize, Guatemala, Honduras, Nicaragua, Paraguay, Marshall Islands, Nauru and Palau.

The United States position emerged following talks between President Biden and President Jinping-Xi where it was agreed that they would 'abide by the Taiwan agreement'. In formal terms, that means that the United States recognises Beijing rather than Taiwan, acknowledges that Taiwan belongs to China and that there is one China but would oppose forced reunification.

*****

China has reiterated its objective of bringing back Taiwan under its control, and by force, if necessary. As a consequence, Japan and the United States have agreed that that they will co-operate in the event of war breaking out over Taiwan. Japan would offer more military bases to United States forces, where 40,000 troops are already stationed to help halt a Chinese invasion. The US troops already stationed in Japan under its constitution, can, at the moment, only act in self-defence but this would change, despite Russian opposition, in the event of China invading Taiwan.

In a statement from the Japanese Deputy Prime Minister, Taro Aso, Japan has pledged to join with the United States to defend Taiwan in the event of China attempting to invade it. He went on to say that if China invaded Taiwan, then China could pose a threat to Japan's own national security. It was in 2015 that the Japanese Government overturned the rule that forbade its military forces from operating overseas with allies.

China reacted to this statement when Zhao Lijian, a Chinese Foreign Ministry spokesman, claimed that Taro Aso's remarks were 'extremely wrong and dangerous'. China also said that it would make a nuclear attack on the eve of the 2022 Olympics if Japan intervened in Taiwan.

The French President, Emmanuel Macron, has agreed to strengthen security ties with Japan to help curb Chinese expansionism. After a meeting with Japan's

Prime Minister, Yoshihide Suga, a joint statement was issued pledging to work together on defence to preserve a free Pacific. The United States has welcomed French involvement, and French troops took part in exercises on both land and sea close to Japan.

In the meantime, Japan has been preparing for war with China, carrying out their first major military drills for 30 years. The reason for these drills is the raised tension with China over their disputed islands. The Japanese have acquired new jet planes, converted merchant ships into aircraft carriers, and built new destroyers and submarines.

Inevitably, China has become aware of this activity, and made it clear that any conflict would bring destructive consequences for Japan. On top of that threat, China also said that Japan would be unable to do anything without United States support.

*****

Just seventy-six years ago, the United States was at war with Japan and was the most important ally of China and now that situation has been reversed. China has become more and more troublesome in the South China Seas over areas disputed by other countries.

Since the start of 2020, as if the world hadn't had enough to cope with – the Coronavirus pandemic with the vast numbers who have died, been hospitalised, lockdowns, effect on economies – the media has been reporting on, at this stage, the ratcheting up of the war of words between China and many other countries. There is now mounting concern over Chinese sabre rattling, including military preparations.

The new President of the United States, Joe Biden, who was sworn in on the 20th of January 2021, in his speech to the Munich Security Conference on the 19th of February 2021 stated that "China's economic abuses and coercion can no longer be tolerated." He vowed to fight back and urged his European allies to prove that 'democracy is not a relic of history' and summed the situation up by saying the rivalry was one of autocracy versus democracy.

In January 2021, the US State Department's spokesman, Ned Price, urged China to stop pressuring Taiwan: "We urge Beijing to cease its military, diplomatic and economic pressure against Taiwan and instead engage in meaningful dialogue with Taiwan's democratically elected representatives."

President Biden was concerned at the growing power of China citing it as the principal threat to the American-led global order and promised to stop China becoming the leading superpower. He condemned "China's opaque financial rules, which drew a veil over 'corruption' and suspect corporate governance." In his speech, he held out a hand to the Chinese Government saying "On the one hand, China is a competitor, but on the other, we need China to settle global problems such as climate change, biodiversity and others. In recent years, China has gained more power on the international stage, and we as the transatlantic alliance, and the democratic countries need to react to that."

*****

The Chinese Navy and Airforce have continued to encroach on Taiwan. For example, on the 21st of January 2021, the Reuters News Agency reported that six Chinese fighter aircraft, together with a US Airforce reconnaissance plane, had entered the South-Western corner of Taiwan's air defence identification zone.

The Chinese missions coincided with a U.S. aircraft carrier group entering the South China Sea for what the U.S. military termed a routine deployment. In the run-up to this incident, China toughened its language towards Taiwan, warning after it stepped up military activities, that 'independence means war' and that its armed forces were acting in response to provocation and foreign interference.

This was the first time Taiwan had mentioned the presence of a U.S. aircraft since it began almost daily reports of Chinese activity in its defence zone in mid–September 2020. Taiwan rarely acknowledges U.S. activity near it, which usually takes the form of U.S. warships sailing through the Taiwan Strait, though diplomatic and security sources say there are frequent U.S. air and naval missions close to the island.

It is estimated that during 2020, there were 380 occasions when Chinese air force planes entered Taiwan's defensive airspace and this figure demonstrated the increasing military tensions. The incursions by Chinese planes, together with coordinated disinformation campaigns represent psychological warfare designed to wear down the Taiwanese people.

In September 2021, while a US warship sailed through the South China Sea, China sent 19 nuclear bombers into Taiwan's airspace on what was claimed as an invasion war game. Taiwan responded by scrambling its combat aircraft, issuing radio warnings and deploying air defence missile systems to monitor the Chinese activity. China said that Taiwan should be 'trembling' as the US won't protect its islands. This comment is interesting because it comes after the US, and therefore its allies, chaotic withdrawal from Afghanistan.

In response to the United States and Canada sending warships to the Taiwan Strait, China reacted by putting out a statement:

"The United States and Canada colluded to provoke and stir up trouble seriously jeopardising peace and stability of the Taiwan Strait."

The United States response was clear:

"This demonstrates the commitment of the United States and our allies and partners to a free and open Indo-Pacific."

*****

The United States has also criticised the Chinese flights. Over the decades since the Chinese Nationalists took over Taiwan, there have been tensions between China and the United States. The United States has no official diplomatic ties with Taiwan, but it is a supporter of Taiwan and is its main provider of weapons.

In a demonstration of its support for Taiwan, the United States deployed twenty-five of its F-22A Raptor stealth fighters and ten F-15E jets to take part in an exercise in July 2021, named Operation Pacific Iron in what China views as an area of its military domination. The US jets will operate from Guam, a United States island territory and from one of the Northern Mariana Islands, from where the planes carrying the atomic bombs had taken off during World War Two. The purpose of this deployment is to demonstrate that the US planes can fly from remote airfields and that if Guam is attacked by China's onshore ballistic missiles, the United States has a response.

In the face of rising military tensions, the Taiwanese Government have appealed to the United States to bring forward the delivery of sixty-six F-16 fighter aircraft. The reason for this request was to boost the island's air defence against what it sees as the increasing threat from China. The sale was approved by President Trump in 2019, with delivery due in 2023 and 2026 while Taiwan would like them by 2022.

*****

At the same time, China has developed its own advanced military technology and while it is unlikely that either side would initiate outright conflict, there is always the chance of a minor incident occurring that could, in turn, lead to conflict because neither side can be seen to lose face. A report from the Taiwanese think-tank, the Institute for National Defence and Security Research, 'found that in 2020, there were the most incursions by Chinese aircraft since 1996. It said China flew more than 380 sorties that entered the island's air defence identification zone'.

China appears relaxed about sending its air force planes into Taiwan's airspace, yet it was angered when the United States sent the USS Curtis Wilbur, a guided missile destroyer, into the China-controlled Paracel Islands, islands which both Taiwan and Vietnam also claim, in the middle of May 2021, declaring it both unprofessional and irresponsible. As far as the United States was concerned, its ship was on a freedom of navigation operation to challenge China's claim to the entirety of the archipelago concerned.

A spokesperson for the PLA said it was an illegal entry and that its forces were mobilised to 'track, warn and expel' the United States warship which was violating China's sovereignty and security and undermining peace and stability in the region. China warned that by sending its warship, the United States was thereby increasing the risk of 'misunderstanding, misjudgement, and maritime accidents'.

The United States issued a statement which said that the USS Curtis Wilbur was upholding 'the rights, freedoms, and lawful uses of the sea recognised in international law by challenging the unlawful restrictions on innocent passage imposed by China, Taiwan, and Vietnam, and also by challenging China's claim to strait baselines enclosing the Paracel Islands'.

In September 2021, tensions heightened when the United States sent a guided missile destroyer through the South China Sea. China had passed a law to assert ownership over international waters that the rest of the world, and an international court, did not recognise.

China claimed that the presence of USS Benfold was 'a violation of its national sovereignty'. China had recently passed a law that demanded foreign vessels submit notice before entering Chinese waters. The USS Navy said that China's claim 'was false and a part of its campaign to misrepresent lawful maritime navigation' and it had certainly not asked for permission to enter the South China Sea.

In response, China, in September 2021, sent a taskforce of warships to patrol the waters off Alaska, a United States Exclusive Economic Zone (EEZ), thereby increasing the tension with the United States which boiled down to 'you did it to us, now we are doing it to you'. The Chinese taskforce was made up of, what was believed to be, two guided missile destroyers, a surveillance ship and a supply vessel.

The editor of the Chinese Global Times had a week before the 'incursion' said:

"Hopefully, when Chinese warships pass through the Caribbean Sea or show up near Hawaii and Guam one day, the US will uphold the same standard of freedom of navigation. That day will come soon."

He then went on to say:

"The era when the US ships one-sidedly declare 'freedom of navigation' in China's near seas will be replaced by a new era in which Chinese and US battleships will reach near each other's territorial seas.

There will be a transition of several decades, but eventually, China and the US, under brand new conditions, and through comparisons, will reach a rule of equity to ensure maritime safety."

America's EEZ does not have full sovereignty over the sea that extends some two hundred miles off its coast, but it has the rights for what is below the surface of the sea.

Wei Dongxu, a military expert based in Beijing, was reported in the Global times to have said that warships from the US:

"Have been making frequent provocations near China in the name of freedom of navigation and now it might feel a little uncomfortable to see China's warships on its doorstep."

The US Pentagon's response was more considered, claiming that it had no objection to foreign vessels sailing in international waters 'even those adjacent to the US'.

*****

The United States isn't the only country that sends warships on freedom of navigation operations. The Times on the 27th of February 2021 carried an article under the headline: *Royal Navy to defy China with patrols in disputed waters*. The purpose of these patrols was to demonstrate that Britain's defence strategy was tilting towards the Indo-Pacific region where the Royal Navy will have a regular presence in the future. The Chief of the Defence Staff, General Sir Nick Carter, said that China was a growing power and as a result, one of Britain's two new aircraft carriers, HMS Queen Elizabeth, would set off on its maiden voyage as the centerpiece of a carrier strike group in May 2021 and would reach East Asia by late summer.

The aircraft carrier has eight RAF and ten US Marine Corps F35B stealth fighters onboard and will be accompanied to Asia by 'six Royal Navy ships, 14 naval helicopters and a company of Royal Marines'. (BBC News, the 3rd of May 2021) The Carrier Strike Group will also be joined by the US destroyer 'The Sullivans' and the Dutch frigate, HNLMS Evertsen. Colonel Simon Doran, the senior US representative said that 'it sends a message to potential adversaries'.

The plan entailed HMS Queen Elizabeth conducting 'freedom of navigation' patrols in the disputed waters of the South China Sea 'amid rising tensions with Beijing'. Once the carrier strike group has passed through the South China Sea, it will then take part in exercises in the Philippine Sea with ships from Australia, France, Japan, New Zealand, South Korea and the United States. It doesn't require much thought to predict how China will view such exercises.

General Carter said that the deployment of HMS Queen Elizabeth was principally about prosperity but also about 'making sure the international rules-based system…is adhered to where it possibly can be'. Britain, he said, wants to make sure that 'global trade can happen in an effective way' because as the population in the region continues to grow, then that is where the markets will be. Realistically, he acknowledged that China would be a rival in some areas but in others, Britain could cooperate with Beijing and that would represent a strategic challenge.

British military chiefs were anticipating that HMS Queen Elizabeth would come under cyberattacks from China in an attempt to jam signals, phishing attacks, and spreading false information in countries where the ship would dock in East Asia. A retired military officer said there 'would be a severe threat from so-called grey-zone attacks, which fall short of war. China is likely to try and interfere with the deployment through cyberattack. You can have a damaging effect below the threshold of conflict'.

Another source said that China could disseminate false information, generating hostility or adverse press, or spread fake stories about sailors acting badly. The Royal Navy was confident that the carrier had the means to defend itself, including sophisticated firewalls and secretive defensive measures. Another source said, 'China will engage in disinformation operations during the deployment in an attempt to weaken resolve and undermine alliances.'

The UK Government has now agreed that once HMS Queen Elizabeth and its escort ships have passed through the South China Sea, it will permanently deploy two warships to that region.

Meanwhile, China has denounced the presence of the British Fleet 'as a pretentious act of neo-colonial chest thumping'. China has also said that its navy would be holding exercises in two separate areas of the South China Sea and said, via the Chinese Global Times, that the navy would, 'closely monitor the UK warships' activities, stand ready to deal with any improper acts, and also see this as a chance for practice and for studying the UK's latest warships up close'.

The UK's Defence Secretary, Ben Wallace, emphasised that the UK had a legal right to sail through the strategic South China Sea as trade to the value of $5 trillion as it passes through it.

*****

Meanwhile, Taiwan was heightening tensions by accusing China of posing 'a grave threat' to peace and stability and calling upon 'nations to confront Beijing'. Taiwan stated that it 'welcomed the carrier's deployment to the region'. Adding that Taiwan would defend itself 'to the very last day', if attacked by China.

John Healey, Labour's Shadow Defence Secretary, accused China of 'challenging maritime freedoms in the South China Seas'. An example of this was when HMS Albion sailed close to the Paracel Islands in 2018. China responded by sending a frigate and two helicopters in an attempt to escort HMS Albion out of the area, which happens to be one of the world's busiest shipping routes. The efforts of the Chinese failed and HMS Albion continued on its way.

*****

However, despite the military and political antagonism, there is another side of the coin. An article on the CNN Travel website, on the 3rd of March 2021, under the heading *Tanks, Propaganda and Tourists*, recounts the story of Taiwan's Kinmen Islands. A broadcast tower, the Beishan Broadcast Wall, complete with 48 large speakers can be found on a hilltop on the North-West tip of Taiwan's Kinmen Islands. The tower was built in 1967 and was an important facility in the Cold War between mainland China and Taiwan. The tower's speakers were used to blast songs by Taiwanese singers, propaganda speeches and even invites to Chinese soldiers to defect, across a ten-kilometer stretch of sea towards the mainland Chinese city of Xiamen, which in due course returned the favour.

Yet despite the political and military differences between China and Taiwan, something strange is going on. Kinmen was under Taiwan's military administration for forty-three years, relying on some 100,000 soldiers to keep its economy afloat. In the early 1990s, the broadcasts came to an end and Kinmen has, since 2001, become a tourist destination for mainland Chinese who made up 41 percent of the 2.5 million tourists who visited it in 2019. The tourism had been made possible due to the implementation in 2001 of what is known as the 'Mini Three Links' involving the start of limited transportation by sea and air, and postal and trade relationships between China and Taiwan.

*****

Formed in 1948, The Peoples' Liberation Army (PLA) is the largest standing army in the world with 2,300,000 active personnel in 2017 and has gained fighting experience from participation in the Chinese Civil War, World War II and the Korean War. In addition to its personnel, it had 6,457 combat tanks, 4,788 armoured fighting vehicles, 1,710 self-propelled artillery, 6,246 towed artillery and 1,770 rocket projectors (The Indian Express, the 16th of July 2017).

The Chinese Air Force was formed in 1949 and is now the largest air force in Asia. The Chinese Airforce is in the process of phasing out its old aircraft and has commissioned a huge number of fighter jets and multi-role aircraft. In 2017, the Chinese defence budget allocation was $152 billion. In 2017, according to the Indian Express, the Chinese Airforce had 1,271 fighter aircraft, 1,385 attack aircraft, 782 transporters, 352 trainer aircraft, and 912 helicopters of which 206 are attack helicopters.

Meanwhile in 2017, the Chinese Navy had 1 aircraft carrier, 51 frigates, 35 destroyers, 35 corvettes, 68 submarines, 220 patrol craft, and 31 mine warfare vessels.

The article in the Indian Express also reported that according to the Arms Control Association, China has a nuclear stockpile of 270 weapons, however, there is no authoritative data available on the number of deployed nuclear weapons. China also has Intercontinental Ballistic Missiles (ICBM) which would enable it to strike targets as far away as 15,000 km. This means that China could strike the United States (11,145 kilometres/6,925 miles) and the United Kingdom (7,780 kilometres/4,846 miles).

In addition, the Chinese Missile Shield guards it from any incoming missile threats by intercepting them before they reach Chinese territory. China has at least ninety ICBMs, out of which sixty-six are land-based. Twenty-four are submarine-based with JL-2 submarine capable of launching ballistic missiles (SLBMs).

In October 2021, it was reported that China had spent an extra £151 billion on military spending this year, meaning a 6.8 percent increase. China has now fired, in August 2021, a hypersonic missile around the globe which ended up missing its target by some twenty miles. This has caused consternation within the United States military which has said that it only increases tension while its Disarmament Envoy said that he 'doesn't know how we can defend against Chinese technology'. In 2018, the United States Congress was told that the United States couldn't defend itself against hypersonic missiles: 'We don't have any defence that could deny the employment of such a weapon against us.' The United States is now spending over $1 billion a year in an effort to catch up with China and Russia because by 2030, the United States and its allies would find that their advantage in aircraft carriers would become a thing of the past.

China, in turn, has warned the United States that its military is 'unstoppable'.

*****

At a press conference after a Nato summit in June 2021, its Secretary-General, Jens Stoltenberg, stated that China 'is changing the nature of warfare'. He went on to say that China is investing heavily in military technology such as robots, facial recognition software and artificial intelligence and thereby posed a threat to Nato, adding that Russia was posing similar threats.

Stoltenberg is concerned that China is increasing its stockpile of nuclear weapons. He wants China to sign-up to those international treaties, along with the United States and Russia which limit the growth of nuclear weapons. Stoltenberg, at Nato's Annual Arms Control Conference, said:

"As a global power, China has global responsibilities in arms control. And Beijing too, would benefit from mutual limits on numbers, increased transparency, and more predictability. These are the foundations for international stability."

In 2020, China was invited to join the START Treaty (Strategic Arms Reduction Treaty) between Russia and the United States which binds the two countries to halve their nuclear stockpiles and the treaty was extended to 2026 – China refused. China's argument was that its nuclear stockpile was smaller than Russia's and the United States and saw it as an attempt to further reduce its nuclear forces.

China is, though, a signatory to the Non-Nuclear Proliferation Treaty by which the 'five formally nuclear weapon states' agreed to stop other countries acquiring them.

*****

According to Reuters (the 1st of September 2021), Taiwan has voiced concerns that China can paralyse its defences according to its Defence Ministry. The Taiwanese Defence Ministry presented its annual report to its Parliament which said that China can launch:

'Soft and hard electronic attacks, including blocking communications across the western part of the first island chain, the string of islands that run from the Japanese archipelago, through Taiwan and down to the Philippines.'

It went on to say that China:

'Can combine with its internet army to launch wired and wireless attacks against the global internet, which would initially paralyse our air defences, command of the sea and counter-attack system abilities, presenting a huge threat to us.'

It further reported:

"With precision, missile attacks that can hit anywhere on the island, China is also capable of paralysing Taiwan military command centres and combat capacity of its naval and air forces."

The Taiwanese President Tsai Ing-wen, has made it a priority to build up its defences by building up its defence industry and buying more equipment from the United States, 'the island's most important arms supplier and international backer'.

In August 2021, the American President, Joe Biden, approved the United States first arms deal with Taiwan amounting to £538 million which China condemned as a violation of a US – China commitment to a one-China policy.

In January 2021, the Pentagon and China's People's Liberation Army held their first direct contact since President Biden took office in an effort to maintain open channels of communication between the two militaries. The main objective was to ensure that in the event of an incident, the two militaries could directly communicate with each other and that a senior Chinese officer would take a call from a United States officer in a crisis.

*****

With mounting tension between China and the United States, there has been a ratcheting up of what can be referred to as an arms race. The United States has modified its Tomahawk cruise missile that is 'accurate to within a few feet', in an attempt to nullify the rapidly expanding Chinese Navy. The modified Tomahawk missile 'is being fitted with a maritime target seeking system to track and hit enemy warships from more than 1,500 miles away' and will have the necessary electronics to evade China's anti-missile radar. The United States was determined to stop China achieving military domination in the Indo-Pacific region. The only other nation that the United States has shared the Tomahawk missile with so far, is Britain where the missiles are carried by Royal Navy submarines.

In the meantime, China is building its own assortment of long range, land based ballistic missiles, including a 'carrier killer' with a range of more than 1,300 miles. It is hoped that these missiles will 'deny access to the region by US carrier strike groups if a conflict were to break out'.

To protect against that, the United States and its allies are seeking to increase the number of submarines in an effort to deter China which sees the key to a successful invasion of Taiwan will be by air and sea control. China will inevitably plan for a rapid offensive before the United States and its allies can respond.

The US and its allies, the Quadrilateral Security Dialogue or Quad (United States, Australia, Japan, and India) see submarines as the way to deny China control of the sea. Taiwan is building a further eight submarines, Australia a further twelve, and Japan a new class of attack submarines. The United States is building an extra nine submarines. It is unlikely that any of these will be available before the mid to late 2020s. China is also accelerating its construction of more submarines, bringing the total number to 79, which will result in a larger force than America has by 2030, meaning that the race is on.

Taiwan, in an effort to address the military imbalance between China and its own military, has built a 'carrier killer' and its President has praised the country's defence development capacity which has seen the first of its domestically manufactured warships launched.

> **Quadrilateral Security Dialogue (Quad) was first convened by Japan in 2007 in response to the 2004 Indian Ocean tsunami. Due to the growth of strategic competition across Asia, the Quad came to an end in 2008 but was reborn in 2017 to 'secure a rule-based order in the Indo-Pacific'.**
>
> **The Quad is maintained by semi-regular summits, information exchanges and military drills between member countries.**

China sees the Quad as just a vehicle to thwart Chinese interests, and Chinese diplomats have accused it of having a cold war mentality based on outdated views of the world. The Chinese Foreign Ministry spokesperson, Hua Chunying, has said, where the Quad is concerned, that: "China opposes certain countries' efforts to form an exclusive clique, portray China as a challenge, and sow discord between regional countries and China."

That statement was rebuffed by the Japanese Ambassador to the United States, Koji Tomita, who said: "The Quad is not about an embryonic defense arrangement directed towards any country, including China. It is a vehicle to realise our shared values and principles in the broader Indo-Pacific."

The members of the Quad have to balance their political and potentially military opposition to China with the fact that China represents an important trading partner.

And to further add to the tensions, China has announced that it has developed, according to the Chinese magazine 'Modern Weaponry', a stealth bomber that is capable of evading radar and can reach the United States territories. The bomber can carry both nuclear and conventional cruise missiles and can travel 5,000 miles before it needs refueling. The Chinese have called this Xian H-20 bomber, 'the god of war in the sky'.

*****

On the 30th of March 2021, it was reported that China had once again breached Taiwan airspace with twenty-five warplanes and on the following day, Taiwan displayed its first amphibious warship, a 10,000–ton ship named Yu Shan. This warship will enable Taiwan to land troops and supplies on those islands that are under threat. The warship is a response to China's increasing threat to re-take Taiwan and it will be armed with cannon, anti-aircraft missiles and Phalanx close-in weapons systems. In addition, Taiwan is upgrading a runway on Pratas Island in the South China Sea which will allow it to fly in military assets and support its army.

Shortly after the Taiwanese announcement, the Chinese Government responded with a public announcement of its own. The Chinese President, Xi, revealed that China had itself built three new warships – an amphibious helicopter carrier, a guided missile cruiser and a nuclear-powered submarine. The amphibious helicopter carrier, named 'Hainan', could well be used in the taking of Taiwan as it can be used for both amphibious and airborne attacks as it can transport 1,200 troops, dozens of helicopters and jump jets. The three new warships acting together would pose a considerable risk to Taiwan and its allies.

China realises that any conflict will involve warships and so it is developing drones that can operate underwater and can attack enemy ships without human involvement.

Joseph Wu's comments came as the Taiwanese minister in charge of the Coast Guard warned China its drones could be destroyed if they strayed too close to Taiwanese territory. As tensions continue to rise, Japan has begun preparing for possible conflict and is seeking greater cooperation with the United States. One of the ways that the United States is helping Taiwan is by sending American Marines and Special Forces soldiers to Taiwan to train its troops.

*****

The PLA's 73rd Armoured Group Army, stationed in Xiamen in Fujian province, is thought to be China's main invasion force if it moves against Taiwan, and has carried out exercises including amphibious landings, artillery drills and urban warfare exercises. It also has drones which will operate in packs just like German submarines did against the Atlantic convoys in the Second World War and will mean that enemy ships can be attacked from many positions. Not surprisingly, other countries have developed their own drones, flying and underwater – particularly the United States and Russia.

In addition, it was reported that China is strengthening three of its airbases nearest to Taiwan – Longtian, Huien, and Zhangzhu – in what is seen as China preparing for World War Three. The Taiwanese coastline opposite these airbases, which range from 140 miles to 250 miles, is rugged with steep cliffs. As a result, there are only thirteen beaches available for military landings which the Taiwanese have strengthened into killing zones.

*****

In response to the increasing tensions in the Far East, China is seeking to establish Atlantic naval bases, for submarines and warships, on the coast of West Africa. China has established economic and trade connections with many African countries that has allowed it to establish, what is known as the 'String of Pearls', a number of ports and fortified islets. Although China could hit the United States with its missiles fired from the Pacific, the establishment of an Atlantic base would make it far easier, due to the shorter distance involved, to strike not only the United States but also its Western Allies. The United States and Nato see this development as China putting pressure on them in response to the increasing tensions surrounding Taiwan.

A Chinese magazine, the Global Times, reported that China was preparing to deploy its new stealth fighter on its next generation of aircraft carriers, throwing down a fresh challenge to the United States and its allies. China already has a stealth fighter, but this new plane is lighter and therefore, more suited to be deployed on aircraft carriers to take on the F-35 Lightening II stealth jet found on British and United States aircraft carriers.

*****

131

Other countries in the Far East have had to deal with Chinese incursions into their territory. Tensions have continued to rise between the Philippines and China. Late in April 2021, the Philippine Government asked China to order 220 fishing boats to leave the area because it suspected the boats were manned by military personnel: 'shadowing, blocking, dangerous maneuvers, and radio challenges'. The Philippine Government also voiced its concerns over the 'incessant, illegal, prolonged and increasing presence of Chinese fishing vessels and maritime militia vessels in Philippine maritime zones', an area over which it sees China as having 'no law enforcement rights'.

In 2016, the Permanent Court of Arbitration sitting in The Hague, dismissed China's claims to the rocks and reefs close to the Philippines but this is not, unsurprisingly, a decision that China accepts. The original case was brought to the Court in 2013 by the Philippines after infringements to its sovereignty by China.

The South China Sea is one of the busiest waterways in the world and is a significant gateway for trade and merchant shipping. The South China Sea is thought to have significant oil and gas reserves and is a route for about £3.4 trillion in trade. There are giant fisheries and lanes for half of all commercial shipping. The run-up to the ruling was fraught with China warning the United States against making any moves that would infringe on China's sovereignty. China, in a show of force, conducted military drills, deploying at least two guided missile destroyers and a missile frigate to demonstrate what its President, Xi Jinping, meant, when he vowed to resolutely defend China's interests in the region.

Despite the Court's ruling, which China has ignored claiming that China's sovereignty over the South China Sea is indisputable. The Chinese have continued to send dredging ships to pour sand on coral reefs to turn them into islands. On these islands, the Chinese military has installed missile launchers, runways, barracks and other security facilities. There is a risk that conflict could ensue as China ignores the ruling while it views other countries using the South China Seas as interlopers Conflict broke out in the 1970s and 1980s, between China and Vietnam, resulting in dozens of deaths and several sunken ships. Therefore, along with Taiwan, the South China presents another issue that could lead to conflict.

The United States has made it clear that if China attacks the Philippines, then it will come to its aid. Antony Blinken, the US Secretary of State, made the following statement in July 2021:

"The People's Republic of China continues to coerce and intimidate South-East Asian coastal states, threatening freedom of navigation in this critical global throughway.

We call on the PRC to abide by its obligations under international law, cease its provocative behavior and take steps to reassure the international community that it is committed to the rules-based maritime order that respects the rights of all countries, big and small.

We also reaffirm that an armed attack on Philippine armed forces, public vessels or aircraft in the South China Sea would invoke US mutual defence commitments under the 1951 US – Philippines Mutual Defence Treaty."

At the same time, the United States had sent USS Benfold through the South China Sea on yet another freedom of navigation operation to reassert the right of free passage in international waters. It, inevitably, upset the Chinese, provoking a statement from the People's Liberation Army:

"The US military's actions have seriously violated China's sovereignty and security, undermined peace and stability in the South China Sea region, and severely violated international law and the norms of international relations.

We urge the US to immediately stop such provocative actions and strictly control maritime and air military activities, or the US will bear all consequences."

The United States Navy responded:

"Under international law as reflected in the Law of the Sea Convention, the ships of all states, including their warships, enjoy the right of innocent passage through the territorial sea.

By conducting this operation, the United States demonstrated that these waters are beyond what China can lawfully claim as its territorial sea and are inconsistent with international law."

*****

China has also caused unrest in Samoa by building new government offices in Apia, the Samoan capital, and a hospital and roads. The result is that forty percent of Samoa's national debt is owed to China. Of particular concern is

China's commitment to build a wharf which will be potentially the largest in the Pacific area and could accommodate twelve large vessels. While Samoa is concerned, the members of the Quad are just as concerned because such a wharf could be used by the Chinese Navy in the event of conflict.

Parliamentary elections in Samoa resulted in Naomi Mata'afa, who is anti-Chinese, having a one vote majority in the 51 seat Parliament, however, she was stopped from being sworn in as Prime Minister by the incumbent Prime Minister, Tuilaepa Sailele Malielegaoi, a pro-Chinese politician, largely due to her commitment to stop the wharf being built. Samoa's ceremonial head of state then refused to convene Parliament thereby thwarting the new Prime Minister from being sworn in despite the Chief Justice in the Supreme Court ruling such action as unlawful. At the time of writing, the stand-off continued.

Eventually, after a period of 100 days, Naomi Mata'afa was finally sworn-in with every intention of stopping the wharf being built.

China has a history of reclaiming several reefs over the years and then fortifying them by building airstrips and 'equipping them with fighter jets and missiles'. In 2016, an international tribunal 'invalidated China's claim to 90% of the South China Sea' but unsurprisingly, China does not recognise that ruling and in the spring of 2021, it has gone on to enrage Japan by ramping up its coastguard patrols around the Senkaku Islands. These uninhabited islands are also claimed by China as Diaoyu, and by Taiwan as Diaoyutai. Since taking office in 2021, President Joe Biden has reiterated Washington's opposition to 'any unilateral action that seeks to change the status quo or to undermine Japan's administration of these islands'.

China is to spend £340 million pound to build an airport on reclaimed land in the Taiwan Strait. The airport would be built on the islands of Dasha and Xiaosha which happens to be the closest possible point from the mainland to Taiwan. Chinese incursions into Taiwanese airspace are designed to show that China could stop American troops coming to Taiwan's assistance if China decided to invade.

China has announced a number of infrastructure projects to link the mainland and Taiwan arising from its national transport plan all of which have been rejected by Taiwan. Among the proposals is a high-speed railway between the mainland and Taiwan and a motorway connecting China and Taiwan. China has argued that these proposals will ease tourism, however, in the event of it invading Taiwan, these fast links will make invasion easier. The projects are to be completed by 2035 but have been rejected by Taiwan, mindful that China has said that it will take over Taiwan by 2050.

*****

The first talks between America's new Biden Government and China were held in Anchorage in Alaska in March 2021. In the run up to the talks, China made it clear that it was not prepared to bend to the United States. America was determined to promote and defend what it saw as the rules-based order, to which it considered China a threat, citing its behavior towards Hong Kong, Taiwan and the Uighur minority. It also cited cyberattacks against America and 'economic coercion toward our allies'. America's view is that without a rule-based order, the alternative would be 'a world in which might and winners take all and that would be a far more violent and unstable world for us all'. In other words, autocracy would prevail.

China's view is that it follows international law and warned America against pushing its version of democracy through military might. Adding to the tension is the fact that China and Russia have been holding joint naval drills with Iran in the Indian Sea, and that the Russian Foreign Minister, Sergey Lavrov, had been invited for talks in the Southern Chinese city of Guilin. While there, he declared Russia's relationship with Europe was over and 'a new romance with China was just beginning'.

Indeed, President Putin and President Xi agreed to extend their friendship treaty which was agreed in 2001 for a further five years thereby demonstrating unity between their two countries, pledging to support each other in territorial disputes.

Russia has said that it has hypersonic nuclear weapons that are five times faster than any other nuclear missiles and can be launched from a submarine and therefore, wipe out cities in the United States. Again, this is said to look like preparation for World War Three. The United States claims that it has missiles that can travel five times faster than the speed of sound.

China's objective for the talks was to reverse Trump-era tariffs, visa restrictions and limits on American sales to Chinese tech companies. The United States wanted China's help to restrain North Korea's nuclear ambitions and had issues over human rights abuses in Hong Kong and the Chinese province of Xinjiang.

Cui Tian Kai, the Chinese Ambassador to the United States, set the tone for the meeting by saying: "China has no room for compromise or concession on core interests such as sovereignty, territorial integrity, and national unification." The issue of Taiwan therefore remained on the table. A senior American officer was reported to have forecast that China could launch an invasion of Taiwan by 2027; while the Chinese President, Xi, has vowed to annex Taiwan, if necessary, by force, by 2050.

*****

In a sign of its continued military support, the United States Biden Administration is now planning to make its first ever arms sale, including forty self-propelled howitzers, to Taiwan. This development comes at a time when the Taiwanese Government has reported that Chinese warplanes had entered Taiwan's airspace nearly every day in 2021 while China was warning the United States to stay away. China's Deputy Foreign Minister, Le Yucheng, spoke to the Associated Press and said:

"The Taiwan question bears on China's core interests. There is simply no room for compromise. China firmly opposes any form of official engagement between the United States and Taiwan, whether low-level or high-level, official engagement is what we firmly oppose. The United States should not play the 'Taiwan card'. It is dangerous. The one China principle is China's red line. No one should try to cross it.

National reunification of China is an historical process swept along by the tide of history. It will not be stopped by anyone or any force. We will never let Taiwan go independent. We are firmly committed to safeguarding national sovereignty and security and promoting national reunification. We are prepared to do everything we can for a peaceful reunification. That said, we don't pledge to give up other options. No option is excluded."

China's Anti-Secession Law (2005) in Article 8 allows for the 'use of non-peaceful and other necessary measures' to take back Taiwan if it becomes independent, if a major event leads to its independence, or if peaceful unification is no longer possible which stands as a very clear warning to the rest of the world.

*****

On the 27th of April 2021, Newsweek carried an article under the headline 'Australian Official Warns Country to Brace for Curse of War'. The Department of Home Affairs Secretary, Mike Pezzullo, had warned that with the increasing tensions with China, the country should try to find ways to maintain peace but should also begin to prepare for war. The cause of this statement was China's warning to Australia that it had to recognise 'the highly sensitive issue over Taiwan'.

The Chinese Foreign Ministry spokesperson, Wang Wenbin, in response to the Australian Defence Minister, suggesting the possibility of conflict with China over Taiwan could not be discounted, said:

"We are willing to do our best to strive for the prospect of peaceful reunification, but we will never leave any space for Taiwan independence separatist activities in any form.

It is hoped that the Australian side will fully recognise that the Taiwan question is highly sensitive, abide by the one-China principle, be prudent in words and deeds, avoid sending any wrong signals to the Taiwan independence separatist forces, and act in ways beneficial to peace and stability in the Taiwan strait and conducive to China-Australian relations."

Australia maintains a 'one-China' policy on Taiwan, which means it does not recognise the self-governing island as a state. However, it only acknowledges China's position that Taiwan is merely a rebellious province of the People's Republic of China, and still supports Taiwan's participation in international organisations. This ambiguity helps Australia to maintain trade, education and diplomatic ties with Taiwan.

In addition, Chinese diplomats, described Australia as 'sick' according to an article in Newsweek on the 29th of April 2021. Relations between the two countries are said to be at an all-time low. The Australian Prime Minister, Scott Morrison, has called for an independent inquiry into the origins of the Coronavirus pandemic and also announced a $580 million budget for military upgrades. In 2020, the Stockholm International Peace Research Institute reported that Australia's military spending was $27 billion while China's was estimated to be ten times higher, as China is a nuclear power while Australia isn't. This clearly demonstrates that Australia would have to be a player in any alliance formed to oppose China.

At a time when China appears to be preparing to take back Taiwan, is it possible that the pandemic could be an example of germ warfare to weaken those countries who oppose China's intentions? Would China be worried about the impact of the pandemic on its own people if it made taking Taiwan back easier? Did China hype-up the impact on its own people to hide what it had done?

China's Foreign Ministry spokesperson, Wang Wenbin, blamed Australia for the two countries deteriorating relationship caused by its 'crude interference into China's internal affairs' and 'its damaging of China's interests'.

Australia's Head of the Department of Foreign Affairs and Trade, has said that "China expects compromise on key national interest in exchange for dialogue and cooperation" despite Australia's desire to have a constructive relationship with China.

*****

China has also been delighted that rifts have appeared in the Five Eyes spy network, the world's oldest intelligence partnership, comprising the United States, Britain, Canada, Australia and New Zealand. This network originated during the Cold War with the Soviet Union as a means of monitoring and sharing classified intelligence. In May 2020, the alliance agreed to expand its remit to include respect for human rights and democracy and consequently, four of its members condemned the Chinese treatment of the Uighur people in Xinjiang Province, China's suppression of democracy in Hong Kong, and its threat to take back Taiwan. A Chinese Government spokesman reacted by mocking the alliance saying, 'those who dared to harm China's sovereignty would find their own eyes poked out'.

However, the fifth member, New Zealand, has not joined the other four members in facing up to China depite its Prime Minister, Jacinda Ardern, admitting that reconciling the differences with China was becoming more difficult. The thinking behind this is that China is New Zealand's largest export market, however, China is also a large export market for Australia but that hasn't stopped it joining forces with the other members. New Zealand has no plans to leave the alliance, but its actions show that it is drawing a distinction between politics and intelligence. Interestingly, a 2017 intelligence review reported that for every ninety-nine pieces of intelligence received by New Zealand, it in turn contributed just one.

The New Zealand Foreign Minister, Nanaia Mahuta, in a major policy address on the country's relations with China, did not hold back from criticism of China, but also was at pains to note Wellington's desire to be respectful in its dealings with its biggest trading partner. However, Mahuta spelt out New Zealand's resistance 'to an American mission, backed by Britain and of late Australia, to develop the Five Eyes intelligence sharing network into an anti-Chinese alliance'. This clearly upset the remaining Five Eyes allies as they felt that New Zealand was 'ditching principles for fear of economic retaliation'.

As would be expected, China has used the stance of New Zealand's Labour Government to attempt to widen the gaps between the Five Eyes alliance.

*****

China's view is undoubtedly that Britain and the United States, would not want to engage in another war. As stated earlier, however, with rising tensions, a mishap could lead to conflict, as could have been the case with HMS Albion, and if that happened, facing the People's Liberation Army would, for example, be 480,893 United States soldiers and 80,040 British soldiers. The United States has a total of 1,300,000 armed forces personnel while Britain has 150,070.

China sees the posting of a United States aircraft carrier, USS Ronald Reagan, from its base in Japan to the Middle East to support US troop withdrawal from Afghanistan as evidence that the United States cannot deliver on its military commitments to Asia. Undoubtedly, the posting of this aircraft carrier will weaken the United States naval forces at a time when China is ratcheting up tensions in the South China Sea and Taiwan.

In fact, the Chinese media has reported that the Chinese Army says that in the event of a war, it will overwhelm the American troops.

*****

President XI gave a speech on the 100th anniversary of the founding of the Chinese Communist Party and warned that bloodied heads would result from any attempt to "bully, oppress, or enslave China." He went on to say that "a great wall of blood and flesh of the 1.4 billion Chinese population would 'repel foreign forces'."

Interestingly, he claimed that China itself had not "bullied, oppressed or enslaved people in other countries." He promised that China would take full control of Hong Kong and would unify with Taiwan. Where Taiwan is concerned, he went on to say:

"It is an historical task to which the party is firmly committed. It is a common wish of the Chinese people to resolve the Taiwan issue and achieve the total reunification of the motherland.

No one should underestimate the strong determination, the firm will, and the powerful ability of the Chinese people to defend national sovereignty and territorial integrity."

In the Chinese magazine, 'Naval and Merchant Ships', the centenary of the Chinese Communists Party was marked by the release of a provocative video simulating the military invasion of Taiwan. In the video, the start of the invasion is the launching of hundreds of missiles towards Taiwan, thereby taking its forces by surprise. Taiwan's warning system fails, its fighter jets are destroyed before they can take off and eventually, its warships are sunk.

*****

Some politicians in the House of Commons would be prepared to sever trade links with China because of 'national security concerns and China's human rights record', namely the treatment of the Uighurs and the takeover of Hong Kong. Others see it as important to work with China to 'promote technology and investment from China as well as green issues'. Nevertheless, there has been a cooling of relations with China as demonstrated by the decision to 'phase out the use of Huawei kit in Britain's 5G infrastructure by 2027'.

*****

In July 2021, the US Deputy Secretary of State, Wendy Sherman, met the Chinese Foreign Minister, Wang Yi, in Tianjin. Prior to this meeting, China's Vice-Foreign Minister, Xie Feng, stated that China would 'teach the US a lesson' on how to treat other countries and that it should stop portraying 'China as an imaginary enemy'.

Sherman said she talked 'about the US commitment to healthy competition, protecting human rights and democratic values' and the US State Department said that she had raised China's violation of human rights in Hong Kong, Tibet and the Uighurs in Xinjiang. The US Secretary of State, Antony Blinken, has said that 'our relationship will be competitive when it should be, collaborative when it can be, and adversarial when it must be', a statement which Xie Feng saw as 'a thinly veiled attempt to contain and suppress China'.

*****

Why does China want to absorb Taiwan? What difference will Taiwan make to China's overall worth? Taiwan is an island that is 245 miles long, from north to south and 90 miles at its widest point with a population in 2020 of 23,844,566. In 1949 and up to the 1960s, Taiwan's economy was originally based on agriculture but then it started to turn towards industrialisation, initially based on textiles. However, companies started producing electronic equipment and by the 1980s, Taiwan was one of the world's leading producers of computers, and particularly computer chips, and associated equipment. Taiwan also set-up steel and shipbuilding industries but these were never going to dislodge the manufacturing of computers and associated products as the country's top industry.

Therefore, would China by invading Taiwan result in significant economic, cultural or other significant gains? It seems that this is a political/military matter where the principle is the over-riding issue, but at what cost, if it happens? If China attempts to invade Taiwan and the Quad plus Britain and other surrounding countries oppose it, then World War Three is a possibility, particularly as Russia will support China.

Henry Kissinger, a former United States Secretary of State, has given his thoughts on the growing tensions surrounding China. Kissinger is concerned that the 'entire world' could become involved if what is seen as the USA-China confrontation escalates. He fears that it could threaten a nuclear war. President Biden is hoping to boost the alliance between the US and its Pacific allies in the light of China's increasingly aggressive actions in the South China Sea, however, Kissinger fears that the nuclear technology that has now been developed surpasses the bombs that were dropped on Japan in 1945, stating that: "For the first time in human history, humanity has the capacity to extinguish itself in a finite period of time."

Kissinger is particularly concerned that China 'is a huge economic power in addition to being a significant military power' and as a consequence, advocates diplomacy as the way forward seeking co-existence as the alternative would be conflict that 'strains the imagination'.

This was the case in 1958 when tensions over Taiwan led to American generals advocating a nuclear strike against China to force Mao Tse-tung to back down. At that time, China was shelling islands in the Taiwan Strait controlled by the Chinese Nationalists. In 1958, China did not have its own nuclear weapons and therefore, the American generals proposed a strategy to bomb Chinese airfields, however, if that had no effect, approval was sought for a nuclear strike in the knowledge that the USSR would launch nuclear strikes to defend its ally. President Eisenhower would not approve nuclear strikes, however, the use of conventional bombing led to Mao stopping Chinese military activities against Taiwan.

Why won't China drop its One-China policy? It could be that allowing Taiwan to continue as it is will enable the two countries to become trading and diplomatic partners. Unfortunately, China is wedded to its One-China policy and backing down would seem to the Chinese to be a sign of weakness, both internally and externally.

*****

The Chinese state-run newspaper, the Global Times, has argued that investing in China's nuclear programme is necessary to act as a strategic deterrence against the United States. The United States has a list of concerns where China is concerned – Hong Kong, Taiwan, Covid–19, and accusations of genocide against the Uighur Muslims – which has strained relations between the two countries. China does not welcome such encroachments on its sovereignty. The rhetoric and military preparations sadly point to only one outcome – **WAR**.

So, what are China's options? If it was just Taiwan, China would win hands-down given the strength of its armed forces. However, if the United States and Taiwan's other allies choose to get involved then it really depends on how that would play out.

*****

However, China has been able to exploit an event that has dominated the news media in August 2021. Those reading this book may be able to remember that in April of 1975, as the North Vietnamese troops approached the southern capital of Saigon, the United States President Ford ordered the evacuation of all Americans and 'at risk' Vietnamese from the country and as a result, more than 7,000 people were evacuated by helicopter from various points in Saigon. Forty-six years later in April 2021, President Biden ordered the withdrawal of American troops from Afghanistan and set a date of 11 September for its completion. The date for completion was later shortened to 31 August.

The withdrawal of American troops inevitably led to the evacuation of troops from other countries such as Britain and other Nato members together with diplomats and those Afghans who had worked for the Allies. In order to secure the evacuation, President Biden sent a further 3,000 troops to Kabul Airport.

The impact on the Afghan Army – its weaknesses, its dependence on US air support, and the negative effect on its morale – did not seem to have been taken account of. Many Afghan soldiers just ditched their uniforms and walked away from their roles. The scenes from Kabul Airport have clearly shown the chaos that has ensued and many Afghans, young and old, male and female, have been killed as a result.

China has relished using President Biden's decision and the ensuing chaos to cause concern for the United States allies in the Pacific region. China's Global Times has warned Taiwan, and additionally, Japan and South Korea, that they could similarly face the United States abandoning its allies.

President Biden has responded to the argument that the United States could no longer be viewed as a reliable ally:

"We have kept every commitment. We made a sacred commitment to article five of the Nato Treaty that if, in fact, anyone were to invade or take action against our Nato Allies, we would respond. Same with Japan, same with South Korea, and same with Taiwan."

Tony Blair, the former British Prime Minister who ordered British troops into Afghanistan in 2001, has said that the West needs to be prepared for foreign intervention or risk a world dominated by Russia and China.

Some media outlets have though speculated that the American troops withdrawn from Afghanistan could be used to support Taiwan but there is no confirmation of this.

*****

In late August/early September 2021, China made further incursions into Taiwanese airspace for invasion wargames. The Sun newspaper reported that Taiwan's Defence Ministry had reported that ten J-16 and four Su-30 fighter jets, an ant-submarine aircraft and four H-6 bombers, which carry nuclear weapons, had entered Taiwanese airspace. Taiwan responded by scrambling combat aircraft, issuing radio warnings and deploying missile systems to monitor the activity.

Incursions into Taiwanese airspace and the Taiwanese response makes the prospect of war more likely. China has rehearsed the invasion of Taiwan, however, conflict could start through a mistake or an accident.

*****

In September 2021, a new alliance was announced between Australia, Great Britain and the United States (AUKUS) which increased the tension with China and also with their European allies. France announced it had been 'stabbed in the back' while China said that the AUKUS alliance were intensifying the arms race and having a 'cold war mentality'.

The Alliance's main stated objective is to help Australia build eight nuclear submarines, although it will take time to do this. The Alliance will also co-operate over artificial intelligence, quantum technologies and undersea drones. In addition, Australia and the United States have reached an agreement on the rotational deployment of US military aircraft to Australia. Britain will use Australia as a base for its nuclear submarines. Using the Australian base will enable Britain to keep a presence in the Indo-Pacific region because the submarines will be able to use the base for maintenance rather than having to return to Faslane in Scotland.

To do this, Australia decided to rip up a contract it had with France, signed in 2016. The contract was worth £30 billion to France to build a fleet of 12 submarines to replace Australia's existing aging fleet.

China reacted by saying that Australian forces would be the first to die in a Chinese counter-attack and that as a result of the Alliance, Australia would become a nuclear war target. The Chinese Foreign Ministry spokesman, Zhao Lijian, said:

"It seriously damages regional peace and stability, intensifies the arms race and undermines the treaty on the 'Non-proliferation of Nuclear Weapons'."

This Treaty was signed in 1968 and was designed to stop the spread of nuclear weapons and weapon technology, to promote co-operation in the peaceful use of nuclear energy and to further the goal of nuclear disarmament.

China has become more assertive across the region and as a result, the United States and its allies are deepening military co-operation and planning an effective response attempt to invade Taiwan. China is also using the chaos caused by the United States in its withdrawal from Afghanistan by telling Taiwan it should be 'trembling' as the United States won't protect it from a Chinese invasion. The Chinese will be sure to use the divisions caused by the creation of AUKUS which will play into the hands of Russia and China.

Although AUKUS represents a challenge to China, hence its war of words, it's caused China to verbally take on the Quad which poses issues for China both strategically and militarily as they are adding to their military resources to counter Chinese expansionism. Two members of the Quad have already confronted China, India on the Himalayan border and Japan over the disputed Senkaku Islands in the East China Sea.

China has only itself to blame though, as it disputes mineral rich waters in the East and South China Seas, continued cyber-attacks and its continued harassment of Taiwan. Those in power in China should have predicted the response their actions would produce – and the more they stick to their actions, the more other nations, particularly the Quad, will increase co-operation, and increase their military preparedness. China is also suspected of producing bombs containing bacteria, including weaponised coronavirus which would be more difficult to neutralise.

*****

Obviously, win or lose, a conflict over Taiwan would have long-term ramifications for the region. A Chinese victory would severely weaken the United States' position and role in the region, while a Chinese defeat could also be very destabilising and act as a precursor to further conflict.

The United States objective in entering such a conflict would be to demand Taiwan independence, or demand also, that China concedes on some other positions before the war would end. The United States, in all likelihood, would be the first country to get involved while the other allies would observe before joining the conflict.

In such a conflict, there would be the inevitable loss of military hardware –
aircraft, ships, drones, vehicles and missiles. There would be another set of issues
that would be affected – infrastructure, trade and travel being the most important
of them.

The saddest outcome of the conflict to come would be the unnecessary loss
of both military and civilian **LIVES** on both sides!

Taiwan has declared that the tensions with China are the most serious in over
40 years. President Xi has said that when China takes over Taiwan, it would be
under a 'one country, two systems model'. There is a major issue with those
words – Hong Kong. The takeover of Hong Kong was based on the 'one country,
two systems model' with guaranteed freedoms which have now largely been
eroded.

Although China hasn't invaded Taiwan yet, just compare it to the Russian
invasion of Ukraine.

Postscript

**Excerpts from the Address at VJ 50th Anniversary British Legion Parade
and Service for the Final Ending of the War Against Japan.
St Nicholas Parish Church in Alcester, Warwickshire
Delivered by Reverend John Stanfield
The 3rd of September 1995**

What is there to say after 50 years? For all who were involved in the forces or in the vital civilian organisations, great thankfulness for the end of six years, and the end of fighting and fear of bombing at home and return to families after years of separation.

We cannot forget those who did not return, those we were close to, comrades with whom we fought, others remember husbands, brothers, fathers, friends, those who only lived about one third of their lives and those with permanent disablement of body or mind…those 23 names on the memorial at the entrance to this church, the same family names of some here, who have not lived these fifty years. The most poignant memorial in Imphal Burma could be on all our memorials… "For your tomorrow, we gave our today."

Although looking at us now, you may not be able to imagine that we were young once, there was a sense of adventure, chance to escape from home, a chance to see the world.

Underlying these other motives were VALUES which however badly observed, were what we fought for:

TRUTH – falsehood.
JUSTICE – injustice.
FREEDOM – oppression.
COMPASSION – cruelty.
LOVE – hatred.
BROTHERHOOD – enmity.

All the essentials of true life. Peace is not just an absence of strife or war, it describes happiness, well-being and good relationships. The end of the war was a beginning.

The first prisoners of war and internees in camps in North China and elsewhere, were liberated by the US Airforce; they had been held for years with rigid camp disciplines, at last were free but they had to be prepared and acclimatised for peace, the starving brought back to health in body and mind; re-orientated. This was not helped by being woken up at 6:00 a.m. their first free morning by the US loudspeaker playing the latest hit *O what a beautiful morning, O what a beautiful day* (the comments are unrepeatable here).

Our commitment to Peace made in our great sharing the total work of Peacemaking in our relationships with others, in our service in the community and the world.

Appendix 1
Hong Kong War Crimes Trial
(the 17th of Oct. 1946 – 14th of Feb. 1947)

**(Copyright held by Suzannah Linton and HKU Libraries, Hong Kong's
War Crimes Trials Collection Website at http://hkwctc.lib.hku.hk)**

Copyright

Accused

Col. Tokunaga Isao (D1)

Capt. Saito Shunkichi (D2)

Lt. Tanaka Hitochi (D3)

Int. Tsutada Itsuo (D4)

Sgt. Harada Jotaro (D5)

Charge

First Charge, (against all Accused):

"Committing a war crime, in that they, at Sham Shui Po, Hong Kong,
between the 24 January 1942 and the 15 August 1945, when members of the
Prisoners-of-War Camp Staff under the command of the first named accused,
and responsible for the well-being of British, Canadian and Dutch Prisoners-of-
War interned in the Sham Shui Po Prisoners-of-War Camp were, in violation of
the laws and usages or war, together concerned in the inhumane treatment of the
said Prisoners-of-War, resulting in the deaths of some and in physical sufferings
to others."

Second Charge, (against D1 and D2):

'Committing a war crime, in that they, at Sham Shui Po, Hong Kong,
between the 24 January 1942 and the 26 September 1942 or thereabouts, when
Commandant and Medical Officer respectively of all; Prisoners-of-War Camps
in Hong Kong, and responsible for the well-being of British, and Canadian

Prisoners-of-War, in violation of the laws and usages or war, together concerned in the inhumane treatment of the said Prisoners-of-War, resulting in the deaths of some and in physical sufferings to others.'

Third Charge, (against D1, D2 and D3):

'Committing a war crime, in that they, in Kowloon, Hong Kong, between April 1942 and May 1944 or thereabouts, when the accused, Col. Tokunaga Isao and the accused, Capt. Saito Shunkichi were respectively, Commandant and Medical Officer of all Prisoners-of-War Camps in Hong Kong and the accused, Lt. Tanaka Hitochi was Commandant of the Upper Argyle Street Officers Camp, and responsible for the well-being of British, and Canadian Prisoners-of-War serving on the medical staff and/or receiving treatment at the said Upper Argyle Street Officer Camp, were, in violation of the laws and usages or war, together concerned in the inhumane treatment of the said Prisoners-of-War, resulting in the deaths of some and in physical sufferings to others.'

Fourth Charge, (against D1 and D2):

'Committing a war crime, in that they, in Kowloon, Hong Kong, between February 1942 and the 16 June 1942 or thereabouts, when Commandant and Medical Officer in Hong Kong, and responsible for the well-being of British, and Canadian Prisoners-of-War serving on the medical staff and/or receiving treatment at the Indian Military Hospital at Argyle Street, Kowloon, Hong Kong, were, in violation of the laws and usages of war, together concerned in the inhumane treatment of the said Prisoners-of-War, resulting in the deaths of some and in physical sufferings to others.'

Fifth Charge, (against D1 and D2):

'Committing a war crime, in that they, in Kowloon, Hong Kong, between the 24 January 1942 and the 15 August 1945 or thereabouts, when Commandant and Medical Officer of all Prisoners-of-War Camps in Hong Kong, and responsible for the well-being of British and Canadian Prisoners-of-War serving on the medical staff and/or receiving treatment at the Bowen Road Hospital, Hong Kong, were, in violation of the laws and usages of war, together concerned in the inhumane treatment of the said Prisoner-of-War, resulting in the deaths of some and in physical sufferings to others.'

Sixth Charge, (against D1 and D2):

'Committing a war crime, in that they at the Prisoners-of-War Camp HQ's at Forfar Street, Kowloon, Hong Kong, in or about the month of August 1942, when Commandant and intelligence officer respectively, of the Prisoners-of-War Camp Headquarters, were in violation of the laws and usages of war, together concerned in the maltreatment of Sgt. J.O. Payne, L/Cpl G. Berzenski, Pte. J.H. Adams and Pte. P.J. Ellis, all Canadian Prisoners-of-War then in their custody and command.'

Seventh Charge, (against D1):

'Committing a war crime, in that he, on or about the month of August 1942, when Commandant of all Prisoners-of-War Camp in Hong Kong, was, in violation of the laws and usages of war, concerned in the killing of Sgt. J.O. Payne, L/Cpl G. Berzenski, Pte. J.H. Adams and Pte. P.J. Ellis, all Canadian Prisoners-of-War then in their custody and command.'

Eighth Charge, (against D1):

'Committing a war crime, in that he, at Hong Kong on or about 14 September 1942, when Commandant of all Prisoners-of-War Camps in Hong Kong, was, in violation of the laws and usages of war, concerned in the killing of Pte. V. Branson, L/Cpl. W.G. Byrne, P. Connely, Pte. J. Steppworth and Pte. M.T. Dunne, all British Prisoners-of-War in his custody and command.'

Ninth Charge, (against D1):

'Committing a war crime, in that he, at Hong Kong on or about October 1942 and 15 August 1945, when Commandant of all Prisoners-of-War camps in Hong Kong, did, in violation of the laws and usages of war, misappropriate for his own use and benefit Red Cross supplies of food, medicine, clothes and other comforts intended for the Prisoners-of-War interned in Hong Kong, and further did permit and condone the misappropriation of such Red Cross supplies by his staff.'

Tenth Charge, (against D1):

'Committing a war crime, in that he, at divers places in Hong Kong between 24 January 1942 and 15 August 1945, when Commandant of all Prisoners-of-War camps in Hong Kong, was, in violation of the laws and usages of war, concerned in the beating, torture and unlawful killing of numerous Chinese Civilians in Hong Kong aforesaid.'

Eleventh Charge, (against D3):

"Committing a war crime, in that he, at No. 167 Argyle Street, Kowloon, Hong Kong, in or about the month of August 1943 when Commandant of the Upper Argyle Street Officers Camp and concurrently O.i/c Intelligence Section, Prisoners-of-War Camps Headquarters, was, in violation of the laws and usages of war, concerned in the maltreatment of two unidentified Chinese Drivers and Lt. Haddock and one or more other British Prisoners-of-War then in his custody and command."

Background

This is the leading case concerning the treatment of Allied Prisoners-of-War ('POWs') held by the Imperial Japanese Army in POW camps across Hong Kong, covering the conditions of detention and also maltreatment, including killings.

D1 was at all material times, in charge of all POW Camps in Hong Kong and held overall responsibility for their proper administration. He was prosecuted on charges 1–10 inclusive.

D2 was on the first accused's staff as medical officer in charge of all POW camps. He was prosecuted on charges 1–5.

D3 was Chief of the Intelligence or Information Section and was responsible for the investigation of documents and identity of POWs, he was also, in April 1944, appointed adjutant. He was prosecuted on charges 1, 3, 6 and 11.

D4 and D5 were on the Camp staff. They were only prosecuted on the first charge.

Allegations

The Prosecution argued that, after the consolidation of the occupation of Hong Kong, conditions in POW Camps deteriorated. The conditions were appalling. The senior Japanese officers did little, if anything, to improve matters and the subordinates followed suit. Owing to lack of proper supervision etc. many prisoners died unnecessarily and many were ill-treated when they should never have been. Red Cross supplies were misdirected and misused. Escaping prisoners were shot without trial.

First, Second, Third, Fourth and Fifth Charge, (The General Charges):

These charges were concerned with the alleged ill-treatment of POWs in various camps and hospitals in Hong Kong and with the general administration of them. They covered:
• Inadequate accommodation, sanitation, food and clothing.
• Harsh treatment of sick POWs and failure to provide drugs and other facilities for their treatment.
• Beating and ill-treatment.
• Working parties sent on war work and dangerous projects.
• Inhumane working of POWs when physically unfit.
• Compulsory signing of a parole.
• Collective Punishment.
• General ill-treatment.

Sixth, Seventh and Eighth Charge, (The POWs Escape Charges):

These charges concerned the escape and recapture of four named Canadian POWs and the attempted escape of five named British POWs. The 6th charge concerns the ill-treatment of the Canadians; the 7th charge related to the execution of the Canadians, while the 8th charge related to the execution of the British (who attempted to escape by having dug a tunnel for that purpose but were caught before escaping).

Ninth Charge, (The Misappropriation Charge):

This charge concerned the misappropriation of Red Cross supplies.

Tenth Charge, (The Civilian Ill-Treatment Charge):

This charge concerned the ill-treatment and killing of Chinese civilians by D1. It was alleged that D1 knew and connived at such misdoings such as beatings, shootings and murder.

Eleventh Charge, (The Civilian/POWs Ill-treatment Charge):

This charge also concerned the ill-treatment and killing of Chinese civilians, but by D3.

Defence

The two main lines of defence were, firstly, that the Accused did all they could in the circumstances and secondly, that Superior Orders had to be obeyed. The Accused admitted that minor offences had been committed, but the gravity of the acts was said to be exaggerated by the Prosecution.

First, Second, Third, Fourth and Fifth Charge, (The General Charges):

In general terms, the Defence denied the claim of poor conditions in the camps.

For D1, it was argued that in some instances, the POWs themselves contributed to their own discomfort in that, for example, they traded their messing equipment for cigarettes. The main line of the Defence, was, however, that in spite of the lack of co-operation from other Military Departments, the Accused did all in his power to ameliorate the lot of prisoners.

D2 argued that he was only responsible for supervising the POWs' own medical officers in respect of diagnosis and treatment. He was never responsible for the health of the POWs. It was admitted that the sanitary equipment in its widest sense 'left something to be desired'. But the main line of defence was that he did his best in extremely difficult circumstances.

D3 argued that he was in no position either to control the guards directly all the time or to give orders to interpreters, and therefore, should not to be held responsible for their misdeeds.

D4 and D5 Accused, argued that the Prosecution's case was shaky with insufficient evidence. They admitted assaulting POWs, but they denied these assaults as being as severe as averred by the Prosecution. They also relied on the Defence of superior order.

Sixth, Seventh and Eighth Charge, (The POWs' Escape Charges):

For the seventh and eighth charges, the Accused pleaded the defence of Superior Orders from the Chief of Staff of the Governor-General's Office. They carried out the orders, despite knowing that according to the law, POWs must have a trial before being executed.

Ninth Charge, (The Misappropriation Charge):

The Defence made light of the Prosecution's evidence. Such items that came his way were gifts. Such items came through theft by dock labourers or by POWs selling supplies in exchange for cigarettes etc.

Tenth Charge, (The Civilian Ill-Treatment Charge):

The Defence mainly argued that there was insufficient evidence to support the charge. There was weak, contradictory or exaggerated testimony given by Prosecution witnesses.

Eleventh Charge, (The Civilian/POW Ill-Treatment Charge):

The Defence mainly argued that there was insufficient evidence to support the charge based on weak, contradictory or exaggerated testimony given by Prosecution witnesses.

Judgement Date
14-Feb-1947
Judgement Confirmation Date:
25-Jun-1947
Judgement Promulgation Date:
02-Jul-1947

Judgement
Held:
1. On the first charge:

• D1 was guilty, except that the court found that he held the command of the POW Camp Staff Hong Kong between 31st January 1942 and 15th August 1945 or thereabouts.

• D2 was guilty, except that the court found that he was a member of the POW Camp Staff Hong Kong between the dates as found in the special finding as to the first Accused.

• D3 was guilty, except that the court found that he was a member of the POW Camp Staff Hong Kong between 31 January 1942 and 1 April 1945 and not between 24 January 1942 and 15 August 1945 or thereabouts, and except for the words, 'in the deaths of some'.

• D4 was guilty, except that the court found that he was a member of the POW Camp Staff Hong Kong between April 1942 and 31 August 1945 when he was transferred from POW Camp staff but continued to reside at Sham Shui Po Pow Camp until he finally left Hong Kong at the end of October 1943 or thereabouts, and except for the words, 'in the deaths of some'.

• D5 was guilty, except that the court found that he was a member of the POW Camp Staff Hong Kong between 1 October 1943 and 15 August 1945, or thereabouts and not between 24 January 1942 and 15 August 1945 or thereabouts, and except for the words 'in the deaths of some'.

2. On the second charge:

• D1 and D2 were guilty, except that the Court found that the dates in respect of both these Accused should be between 31 January 1942 and 26 September 1942 or thereabouts and not between 24 January 1942 and 26 September 1942 or thereabouts, and except, in respect of both these Accused, for the words 'in the deaths of some'.

3. On the third charge:

• D1 and D3 were guilty, except for the words 'in the deaths of some'.

• D2 was guilty.

4.   On the fourth charge:

5.   • D1 and D2 were not guilty.

6.   On the fifth charge:

• D1 and D2 were guilty, except that the Court found that these two Accused were respectively Commandant and Medical Officer of all POW Camps in Hong Kong between 31 January 1942 and 15 August 1945 or thereabouts and not between 24 January 1942 and 15 August 1935 or thereabouts.

7.   On the sixth charge:

• D1 was guilty,

• D3 was not guilty.

8.   On the seventh, eighth and ninth charge:

• D1 was guilty.

9.   On the tenth charge:

• D1 was not guilty.

10. On the eleventh charge:

• D1 was not guilty.

Sentence Imposed

D1: death by hanging, commuted to imprisonment of life.

D2: death by hanging, commuted to 20 years imprisonment.

D3: 3 years imprisonment.

D4: 2 years imprisonment.

D5: 1 year imprisonment.

Appendix 2
The Potsdam Declaration Issued
on the Evening of the 26th of July 1945

(1) We, the President of the United States, the President of the National Government of the Republic of China and the Prime Minister of Great Britain, representing the hundreds of millions of our countrymen, have conferred and agree that Japan shall be given an opportunity to end this war.

(2) The prodigious land, sea and air forces of the United States, the British Empire and of China, many times reinforced by their armies and air fleets from the west are poised to strike the final blows upon Japan. This military power is sustained and inspired by the determination of all the Allied nations to prosecute the war against Japan until she ceases to resist.

(3) The result of the futile and senseless German resistance to the might of the aroused free peoples of the world stands forth in awful clarity as an example to the people of Japan. The might that now converges on Japan is immeasurably greater than that which, when applied to the resisting Nazis, necessarily laid waste to the lands, the industry and the method of life of the whole German people. The full application of our military power, backed by our resolve, will mean the inevitable and complete destruction of the Japanese armed forces and just as inevitably, the utter devastation of the Japanese homeland.

(4) The time has come for Japan to decide whether she will continue to be controlled by those self-willed militaristic advisers whose unintelligent calculations have brought the Empire of Japan to the threshold of annihilation, or whether she will follow the path of reason.

(5) Following are our terms. We will not deviate from them. There are no alternatives. We shall brook no delay.

(6) There must be eliminated for all time, the authority and influence of those who have deceived and misled the people of Japan into embarking on world conquest, for we insist that a new order of peace, security and justice will be impossible until irresponsible militarism is driven from the world.

(7) Until such a new order is established and until there is convincing proof that Japan's war-making power is destroyed, points in Japanese territory to be designated by the Allies shall be occupied to secure the achievement of the basic objectives we are here setting forth.

(8) The terms of the Cairo Declaration shall be carried out and Japanese sovereignty shall be limited to the islands of Honshu, Hokkaido, Kyushu, Shikoku and such minor islands as we determine.

(9) The Japanese military forces, after being completely disarmed, shall be permitted to return to their homes with the opportunity to lead peaceful and productive lives.

(10) We do not intend that the Japanese shall be enslaved as a race or destroyed as a nation, but stern justice shall be meted out to all war criminals, including those who have visited cruelties upon our prisoners. The Japanese government shall remove all obstacles to the revival and strengthening of democratic tendencies among the Japanese people. Freedom of speech, of religion, and of thought, as well as respect for the fundamental human rights shall be established.

(11) Japan shall be permitted to maintain such industries as will sustain her economy and permit the exaction of just reparations in kind, but not those industries which would enable her to re-arm for war. To this end, access to, as distinguished from control of raw materials shall be permitted. Eventual Japanese participation in world trade relations shall be permitted.

(12) The occupying forces of the Allies shall be withdrawn from Japan as soon as these objectives have been accomplished and there has been established in accordance with the freely expressed will of the Japanese people, a peacefully inclined and responsible government.

(13) We call upon the Government of Japan to proclaim now, the unconditional surrender of all the Japanese armed forces, and to provide proper and adequate assurances of their good faith in such action. The alternative for Japan is prompt and utter destruction.

Appendix 3
Emperor Hirohito's Pre-recorded Radio Broadcast to the Japanese People, Accepting the Potsdam Declaration

To our good and loyal subjects: after pondering deeply the general trends of the world and the actual conditions obtaining in our empire today, we have decided to effect a settlement of the present situation by resorting to an extraordinary measure.

We have ordered our Government to communicate to the Governments of the United States, Great Britain, China and the Soviet Union that our empire accepts the provisions of their joint declaration.

To strive for the common prosperity and happiness of all nations, as well as the security and well-being of our subjects is the solemn obligation which has been handed down by our imperial ancestors and which we lay close to the heart.

Indeed, we declared war on America and Britain out of our sincere desire to ensure Japan's self-preservation and the stabilisation of East Asia, it being far from our thought either to infringe upon the sovereignty of other nations or to embark upon territorial aggrandisement.

But now the war has lasted for nearly four years. Despite the best that has been done by everyone – the gallant fighting of our military and naval forces, the diligence and assiduity of out servants of the State and the devoted service of our 100,000,000 people – the war situation has developed not necessarily to Japan's advantage, while the general trends of the world have all turned against her interest.

Moreover, the enemy has begun to employ a new and most cruel bomb, the power of which to do damage is, indeed, incalculable, taking the toll of many innocent lives. Should we continue to fight, it would not only result in an ultimate collapse and obliteration of the Japanese nation, but also it would lead to the total extinction of human civilisation.

Such being the case, how are we to save the millions of our subjects, nor to atone ourselves before the hallowed spirits of our imperial ancestors? This is the reason why we have ordered the acceptance of the provisions of the joint declaration of the powers.

We cannot but express the deepest sense of regret to our allied nations of East Asia, who have consistently cooperated with the Empire toward the emancipation of East Asia.

The thought of those officers and men as well as others who have fallen in the fields of battle, those who died at their posts of duty, or those who met death [otherwise] and all their bereaved families, pains our heart night and day.

The welfare of the wounded and the war sufferers and of those who lost their homes and livelihood is the object of our profound solicitude. The hardships and sufferings to which our nation is to be subjected hereafter, will be certainly great.

We are keenly aware of the inmost feelings of all of you, our subjects. However, it is according to the dictates of time and fate that we have resolved to pave the way for a grand peace for all the generations to come by enduring the unendurable and suffering what is unsufferable. Having been able to save and maintain the structure of the Imperial State, we are always with you, our good and loyal subjects, relying upon your sincerity and integrity.

Beware most strictly of any outbursts of emotion that may engender needless complications, of any fraternal contention and strife that may create confusion, lead you astray and cause you to lose the confidence of the world.

Let the entire nation continue as one family from generation to generation, ever firm in its faith of the imperishableness of its divine land, and mindful of its heavy burden of responsibilities, and the long road before it. Unite your total strength to be devoted to the construction for the future. Cultivate the ways of rectitude, nobility of spirit, and work with resolution so that you may enhance the innate glory of the Imperial State and keep pace with the progress of the world.

Appendix 4
The Tripartite Pact Signed
on the 27th of September 1940

ARTICLE 1. Japan recognises and respects the leadership of Germany and Italy in the establishment of a new order in Europe.

ARTICLE 2. Germany and Italy recognise and respect the leadership of Japan in the establishment of a new order in Greater East Asia.

ARTICLE 3. Japan, Germany, and Italy agree to cooperate in their efforts on aforesaid lines. They further undertake to assist one another with all political, economic and military means if one of the Contracting Powers is attacked by a Power at present not involved in the European War or in the Japanese-Chinese conflict.

ARTICLE 4. With a view to implementing the present pact, joint technical commissions, to be appointed by the respective Governments of Japan, Germany and Italy, will meet without delay.

ARTICLE 5. Japan, Germany and Italy affirm that the above agreement affects, in no way, the political status existing, at present, between each of the three Contracting Powers and Soviet Russia.

ARTICLE 6. The present pact shall become valid immediately upon signature and shall remain in force ten years from the date on which it becomes effective. In due time, before the expiration of said term, the High Contracting Parties shall, at the request of any one of them, enter into negotiations for its renewal.

In faith whereof, the undersigned duly authorised by their respective governments have signed this pact and have affixed hereto, their signatures.

Appendix 5
Declaration by United Nations –
the 1ˢᵗ of January 1945

(This work is from an official document of the United Nations).

A Joint Declaration by the United States, the United Kingdom, the Union of Soviet Socialist Republics, China, Australia, Belgium, Canada, Costa Rica, Cuba, Czechoslovakia, Dominican Republic, El Salvador, Greece, Guatemala, Haiti, Honduras, India, Luxembourg, Netherlands, New Zealand, Nicaragua, Norway, Panama, Poland, South Africa, Yugoslavia.

The Governments signatory hereto,

Having subscribed to a common program of purposes and principles embodied in the Joint Declaration of the President of the United States of America and the Prime Minister of the United Kingdom of Great Britain and Northern Ireland dated August 14, 1941, known as the Atlantic Charter.

Being convinced that complete victory over their enemies is essential to defend life, liberty, independence and religious freedom, and to preserve human rights and justice in their own lands as well as in other lands, and that they are now engaged in a common struggle against savage and brutal forces seeking to subjugate the world,

DECLARE:

(1) Each Government pledges itself to employ its full resources, military or economic, against those members of the Tripartite Pact: and its adherents with which such government is at war.

(2) Each Government pledges itself to cooperate with the Governments signatory hereto and not to make a separate armistice or peace with the enemies.

The foregoing declaration may be adhered to by other nations which are, or which may be, rendering material assistance and contributions in the struggle for victory over Hitlerism.

Done at Washington

January First, 1942

The adherents to the Declaration by the United Nations, together with the date of communication of adherence, are as follows:

- Mexico – June 5, 1942
- Philippines – June 10, 1942
- Ethiopia – July 28, 1942
- Iraq – Jan. 16, 1943
- Brazil – Feb. 8, 1943
- Bolivia – Apr. 27, 1943
- Iran – Sept. 10, 1943
- Colombia – Dec. 22, 1943
- Liberia – Feb. 26, 1944
- France – Dec. 26, 1944
- Ecuador – Feb. 7, 1945
- Peru – Feb. 11, 1945
- Chile – Feb. 12, 1945
- Paraguay – Feb. 12, 1945
- Venezuela – Feb. 16, 1945
- Uruguay – Feb. 23, 1945
- Turkey – Feb. 24, 1945
- Egypt – Feb. 27, 1945
- Saudi Arabia – Mar. 1, 1945
- Lebanon – Mar. 1, 1945
- Syria – Mar. 1, 1945

Appendix 6
United Nations General Assembly
Resolution 2758 – the 25th of October 1971

(This work is from an official document of the United Nations).
Restoration of the lawful rights of the People's Republic of China in the
United Nations.

The General Assembly:

1. Recalling the principles of the Charter of the United Nations,

2. Considering the restoration of the lawful rights of the People's Republic of China is essential both for the protection of the Charter of the United Nations and for the cause that the United Nations must serve under the Charter,

3. Recognising that the representatives of the Government of the People's Republic of China are the only lawful representatives of China to the United Nations and that the People's Republic of China is one of the five permanent members of the Security Council,

4. Decides to restore all its rights to the People's Republic of China and to recognise the representatives of its Government as the only legitimate representatives of China to the United Nations, and to expel forthwith, the representatives of Chiang Kai-shek from the place which they unlawfully occupy at the United Nations and in all the organisations related to it.

25 October 1971.

Appendix 7
Smugglers, Spies and Dragon Slayers, Thursday, the 12th of November 2020 | The National Archives | On the Record, Podcasts

(Contains public sector information licensed under the Open Government Licence v3.0.)

The story of Boonpong's wartime actions is taken from the above podcast.

"On 7 December 1941, the Japanese launched their infamous attack on the American naval base at Pearl Harbour, Hawaii, in an attempt to block the U.S. Navy from interfering in their invasion of South-East Asia. The very next day, Japanese forces entered the Kingdom of Thailand, and after five hours of fierce fighting, a ceasefire and an alliance was announced. For Japan, Thailand was a gateway to Burma, Malaya, and –eventually–British India. In order to move soldiers through Thailand, the Japanese began construction on the Burma Railway, which has gone down in history as the Death Railway.

Pad Kumlertsakul: the Thai-Burma Railway was commissioned by Japanese right after they conquered Thailand to supply the Japanese force and ammunition into Burma. So, altogether, more than 60,000 Allied prisoners of war were employed in the construction of this Thai-Burma Railway.

Sarah Castagnetti: This is Pad Kumlertsakul, an Adviser for Defence, Maritime and Environment here at The National Archives. After learning about Boonpong a few years ago, Pad decided to see if we had any records connected to Boonpong in our collections. This began a larger research project into Boonpong's story and the prisoner of war camps along the Burma railroad in the Second World War.

More than 60,000 Allied prisoners of war were forced to work on the railroad. They were mainly from Britain, the Netherlands, and their colonies, as well as Australia, and America. These men were held in POW labor camps along the length of the railroad's intended path. In each camp, a commandant–usually an officer–was chosen from among the prisoners to manage their men and liaise with the Japanese. One such commander was British Lieutenant Colonel Philip John Denton Toosey.

Pad: Documents about Boonpong at The National Archives are very scant. But, luckily, I found one document of this camp commandant. This document is in the investigation file of the War Crimes Group, which is part of the general headquarters of Allied Force South-East Asia. This file was relating to the investigation of Malaya and Thailand prisoners of war camps, a report by Lieutenant Colonel Philip John Denton Toosey. The report of Colonel Toosey had shed some light on the living condition of prisoners of war and how he and Boonpong managed to work together behind the Japanese soldiers.

Sarah: Starting with this first source–Toosey's post-war account of the war crimes he witnessed in Thailand–Pad looked for more information on the story of Boonpong, the Thai shopkeeper turned resistance smuggler that Toosey names in his report. Pad was able to locate relevant oral histories in the collections of the Imperial War Museum as well as from Thai sources, including one from Boonpong's daughter, who worked alongside her father to smuggle supplies into the camps during the war.

Pad: Boonpong, he was a son of a Thai traditional doctor. He was born on the 21st of April 1906. He was the oldest of seven children. After he was finished with high school, he was working at the Siamese Railway Department for eight years before he resigned to work in the business with his brother. Him and his brother opened a shop named 'Boonpong and Brother in Kanchanaburi'. As a shop owner, Boonpong held a position as a mayor of Kanchanaburi, which is the province where the Imperial Japanese army build the bridge on the River Kwai, where the Thai-Burma railway starts.

So, because he was the mayor of Kanchanaburi, his public responsibility brought him into contact with the Japanese troops who were in charge of the building of the Thai-Burma Railway.

Sarah: The Japanese army commissioned Boonpong and his shop to supply food for a number of camps along the railway line in his province. This gave Boonpong access to these camps with very few restrictions.

Pad: Boonpong, at that time, he also worked in secret with a resistance group based in an internment camp in Bangkok. This resistance group was called 'V Organisation'.

According to his daughter's interview, the first-hand experience that Boonpong had when he went into the prisoner of war camp, had a tremendous impact on him as he saw a lot of chronic and acute conditions that the prisoner of war has to endure and maltreatment that the prisoner of war has by their Japanese captors.

Sarah: At about the same time, Colonel Toosey, the camp commandant, was instructed by the Japanese to set up a hospital for the prisoners of war. Conditions in these camps were terrible, and many of the men were dying. But without the prisoners' labour, construction of the railway would be delayed, so the Japanese needed to keep the Allied troops well enough to work.

Toosey and Boonpong met for the first time in July 1943, when they were introduced by a British army interpreter during one of Boonpong's visits to Toosey's camp. Now, Boonpong had access and a contact in the camps.

According to his daughter, Boonpong felt he couldn't just stand by without helping after seeing the horrible conditions in the camp and the immense need for food and medicine. So he and his daughter began the dangerous work of smuggling these supplies into the camp along with other valuable items like batteries for radios.

Pad: If he'd been caught, he will be shot by Japanese or be tortured by the Japanese.

Sarah: This work put Boonpong and his family at risk in more than one way. Not only would they be in grave danger if they were caught, but Boonpong was also spending a lot of his own money to purchase the supplies, a choice that would leave him in a bad financial situation after the war.

Despite the risk, Boonpong continued to smuggle supplies into POW camps along the railway for the rest of the war, up until the Japanese surrender in September 1945 when the Allied POWs were finally freed.

Pad: The work of Boonpong and his daughter, I think, had a tremendous impact on the life of the prisoner of war on the Thai-Burma Railway, because it saved the life of…if not thousands, it's going to be hundreds of prisoners of war. According to Colonel Toosey's account, the death rate before he met Boonpong is about six deaths per day. So, after he [met] Boonpong, that death rate was reduced to three a week. So, it's quite a lot.

Sarah: As for the men he helped, they never forgot Boonpong and what he had done for them. And that's evidenced in the money they raised to solve his financial problems after the war.

Pad: In 1947, Colonel Toosey heard that Boonpong was running a bus company. He got into difficulty, Boonpong got into difficulty. So Colonel Toosey asked his fellow prisoners to contribute the money to help Boonpong. They raised about 40,000. At that time, it's about 60 or how many years, 70 odd years [ago], I think…to help Boonpong and his bus company…and then later on, his bus company becomes successful, and his son runs it, I think, up to 1985, the bus company is still running.

Sarah: Another British POW camp commandant, Colonel Henry Cary Owtram, recommended Boonpong for the prestigious King's Medal for Courage in the Cause of Freedom, which honours foreign nationals who helped allied efforts during the war. And, in a nice connection to our story on St George, Boonpong was also made an officer of a Dutch chivalric order, the Order of Orange-Nassau, in honour of the Dutch prisoners of war whose lives he saved. But despite receiving recognition in the form of medals and honours after the war, his heroic actions weren't well known by the general public during his lifetime.

Pad: He died in January 1982. His story is not very well known until recently, even in Thailand. His work and achievements during the war has become public attention after one of the Thai television channels produced a drama about his life and about his work at that time.

Sarah: But even before the 2013, Thai television drama series generated more wide-spread interest in his story, the soldiers Boonpong had helped were working to keep his memory and legacy of selfless service alive.

This included Colonel Sir Ernest Edward 'Weary' Dunlop, one of the most famous Australian veterans of the Second World War. While he was a prisoner of war in Thailand, Dunlop served as the leader of his camp, just like Colonel Toosey. His was one of the camps helped by Boonpong, and he never forgot it. Before the war, Dunlop trained as a surgeon in Australia, and it was through medicine that he found a way to honour Boonpong.

Pad: In 1985, Edward 'Weary' Dunlop, in his Anzac Day speech in 1985, he has a tribute to Boonpong and other Thai [people] who helped prisoners of war.

After that, in 1986, by the effort of ex-prisoner of war, they have a fellowship funded called the 'Weary Dunlop Boonpong Exchange Fellowship'. This fellowship is for the collaborative program between the Royal Australian College of Surgeons and the Royal College Surgeons of Thailand, to provide the opportunity for Thai surgeons to undertake surgical training in Australia.

Sarah: Dunlop passed away soon after the fellowship was established, but its impact has far outlived him. In 2019, the Weary Dunlop Boonpong Fellowship reached the milestone of 100 Thai medical students sent to Australia on exchange.

Boonpong's service is also mentioned several times in a 1999 collection of articles by Scottish survivors of Japanese POW camps. And in 2008, a documentary on the legacy of Dunlop and Boonpong was released called 'The Quiet Lions'.

Pad: I think his story inspires us and shows us how normal people can do extraordinary things for other people, to contribute to a major impact.

Sarah: I think it says something that even though he's not famous, Boonpong's actions are remembered all over the world by those he helped. Including in Thailand.

Every year, in Boonpong's hometown of Kanchanaburi, the River Kwai Bridge week memorialises the construction of the bridge at the start of the Death Railway and honours the lives lost. In 2017, the highlight of the week's programming was a musical that told Boonpong's story and honoured him as a wartime hero and someone to inspire younger generations." Appendix 8 will show the armed services of the Western Allies compared to China.

Bibliography

Ambrose, H.(2010), *The Pacific. Hell Was an Ocean Away,* Canongate Books Ltd, Edinburgh.

Bailey, R., (2009), *Forgotten Voices of The Secret War. An Inside History of Special Operations During the Second World War,* Ebury Press.

BBC News Website (the 17th of November 2019), *Court Finds UK War Crimes but Will Not Take Action.*

Berliner, P. (1956), *Sir Walter Fletcher,* The Times, London.

Chang, J. (2006), *Mao. The Unknown Story, Vintage Books, London.*

Diwik, A. and Han, J., *The Forgotten Theater of WWII of China-Burma-India. The Untold Story of the First Chinese Expeditionary Force,* Pacific Atrocities Education, San Francisco.

Farrell, T.,(December 2016), *The Chinese Revolution and the Rise of Mao,* Military History Monthly, London.

Foot, M.R.D. (1984), *SOE. The Special Operations Executive 1940–46,* British Broadcasting Corporation, London.

Hansard (the 9th of May 1944), *Economic Warfare.*

Hastings, M. (2007), *Nemesis. The Battle for Japan 1944–45,*Harper Perennial, London.

Holland, J. (2016), *Burma '44. The Battle That Turned Britain's War in the East,* Transworld Publishers, London.

Hsiung, J. (1992), *China's Bitter Victory: War with Japan 1937–1945,* Routledge.

Lewis, J. and Steele, B. (2001), *Hell in the Pacific. From Pearl Harbour to Hiroshima and Beyond,* Channel 4 Books.

Mayer S. L. (Edited by: 1984), *The Rise and Fall of Imperial Japan, 1894–1945,* Bison Books Limited.

Morrison, H. (1985), *A Photographer in Old Peking,* Oxford University Press.

Powers, D. *Japan: No Surrender in World War Two,* ww2.gvsu.edu/wall/Japan NO SURRENDER htm

Pye, L. and Pye M. (1985), *Asian Power and Politics: The Cultural Dimensions of Authority,* Harvard University Press.

Ritter, R. (2014), *China's War with Japan 1937–1945. The Struggle for Survival,* Penguin Books, London.

Stanfield, J., *100 Years of Family Memories. Mostly in China, a Compendium,* Published Privately.

Stanfield, J. and M., (1980), *From Manchu to Mao,* Epworth Press.

Stanfield, J. *Secret War. Special Operations Executive in World War Two 1940 – 1946.*

Stanfield, J, (2012), *War Letters Home. 1941–46 India, SOE, China,* Blurb Creative Publishing Service.

Tsunetomo, Y (2000), *Hagakure. The Book of the Samurai,* Kodansha International Ltd.

Webster, Donovan (2004), *The Burma Road. The Epic Story of One of World War II's Most Remarkable Endeavours,* Macmillan, London.

Wilkinson, P. and Astley, J. B. (2010), *Gubbins & SOE,* Pen and Sword Military.

Index

This book contains so many references to Chiang Kai-Shek and the Chinese Nationalists, Mao Tse-tung and the Chinese Communists and John Stanfield that they have not been included in this Index.

Anti-secession Law (China) 136
Ao, Sosangtemba 84
Aozu Major-general 90
Army Epidemic, Prevention
and Water Supply Unit apanese) 88
Army Group Signals (SEAC) 37
Aso, Taro, Japanese Deputy 117
Atomic Bomb, US Testing 15
Atomic Heritage Foundation 14
Attlee, Clement 48
Australia 137

Biao, Lin 78, 79, 109
Biden, US President Joseph 94
                        118, 119, 128, 143
Blair, Tony 143
Blinken, Antony 116, 133
Brand, Colonel Kenny 47
British Army Aid Group 47, 80
                                  81, 82
British Legation, Peking 102

Carter, General Sir Nick Carter 123
Chen, Duxiu 71
Chenault, General Clair 45, 46, 109

Cheng, Chenault, General
Clair Sun Lien 22
Chou En- Lai 73, 107
Chunking 52, 82
Churchill, Winston 15, 39, 40
                              48, 59, 70

Dalton, Dr Hugh 40
De Wiart, General Sir Adrian ... 103
De, Zhu 72
Dongjo, Fu 110
Donovan, William 44
Doolittle Raid 91

Enbo, General Tang 97
Evans, Captain Adrian 20, 52, 54

Feng, Xie 140
Fleming, Ian 41
Fletcher, Walter 55, 60
Flying Tigers 45, 46
Force 38, 104, 133

Gang, Gao 75
Geneva Convention 90

Great Proletarian Cultures
Revolution 113
Gubbins, Brigadier Colin...... 40, 41
Guotao, Zhang 75

Healey, John 124
Hirohito, Emperor of Japan . 14, 16
68, 69, 86, 89, 90, 92
Hiroshima 16
HMS Albion 139
HMS Queen Elizabeth 123, 124
HNLMS Evertsen 123
Ho, General..................... 20, 52, 54
Hucheng, General Yang 75
Hurley, Patrick........................... 108

Ichi-Go Offensive................. 77, 96
Imai, General Takeo 77
Ing-Wen, President Tsai ... 112, 128
International Criminal Court 93

Japan – Development of
Atomic Bomb 14
Jingwei, Wang 65
Jinping-Xi, President of China . 135
139
Joffe, Adolf................................ 64

Kaiko,General She...................... 89
Killery, Valentine 42
King, Lieutenant Allen 51
Kissinger, Henry....................... 141
Knott, Colonel Jackie 36

Lavrov, Sergey, Russian
Foreign Minister 135
Li, Dai....................................... 43
Li, Dazhao 71
Lijian, Zhao 117
Long March 74

Mackenzie, Colin....................... 57
Macron, President Emmanuel .. 117
Malayan People's Anti-
Japanese Army 47
Manchuria..................... 15, 67, 78
Menzies, Sir Stewart.................. 42
MI9 81
Mikai, Toshiaki 84
Morrison, Hedda.............. 114, 115
Mountbatten, Admiral Lord 53

Nagasaki 16
Nan, Marshal Hu Zang 52, 54
Nanking Massacre 84
National Defence and
Security Research 121
Nemoto, General Hiroshi 22
New Fourth Army Incident 76
New Zealand.................... 138, 139
Noda, Tsyuoshi........................... 84

Office of Strategic Services........ 96
Onoda, Hiroo 18
Operation Kogo 97
Operation Remorse............... 59, 60
Operation Rimau 91
Operation Waldorf..................... 59

Pearl Harbour 69, 76
Permanent Court of Arbitration 132
Potsdam Conference................... 14
Puyi, Emperor...................... 61, 67

Quadrilateral Security Dialogue129

Ride, Professor Lindsay 80
Roosevelt, President 45, 59
67, 70, 99
Saipan 85, 86
Selbourne, Lord......................... 56

Sherman, Wendy 140
Shikai, Yuan 63
Sino-American Co-operation
Organisation 43
Smith, Major Philip 47, 51
Smuts, General............................ 58
Sook Ching Massacre 90, 93
Stalin, Josef............. 14, 15, 79, 108
Stilwell, General Joseph   ..45, 70
                                              76, 99

Stoltenberg, Jens Nato
Secretary General 126, 127
Strategic Arms
Reduction Treaty 127
Suga, Yoshihide........................ 118
Sun, Yat-sen 63, 65

Tojo, General Hideki 68, 84, 85
Tomita, Koji 129
Tripartite Pact 68
Truman, President Harry 15

Unit 1855.................................... 88
Unit 731..................................... 88
United Nations......................... 115
United Nations War Crimes
Commission................................ 93
USS Benfold............................. 121
USS Curtis Wilbur................... 121
USS The Sullivans................... 123

Wedemayer, General 52, 53, 99
Wu, Joseph 116, 130

Xiaoping, Den 113
Xueliang, General Zheng 75

Yi, Wang 140
Yuming, General Du 78

Zhiden, Liu 75
Zongnan, Marshall Hu.............. 101
Zuoyi, General Fu..................... 109